# Get the Cookie, Paco!

VALUABLE LESSONS IN
# LEADERSHIP
FROM MY DOGS

## Andrew Krüger

Middleton Stout Books, Dennis, MA


ISBN 10: 0615524648
ISBN-13: 9780615524641

Library of Congress Control Number: 2011936202
CreateSpace, North Charleston, SC

# Contents

Acknowledgments                                                              xi

Introduction                                                                xiii

**I. WORKING ON YOURSELF**                                                    I

**Chapter 1:** Just Jump In                                                   3

*Acting without complete information*

**Chapter 2:** Fighting the Leash                                            11

*Knowing when to leave well enough alone*

**Chapter 3:** "Don't Worry, We're Coming Right Back!"                       17

*Keeping your mind in the now*

**Chapter 4:** Being Bulldogged                                              23

*Persistence*

**Chapter 5:** Rebranding a Pit Bull                                         29

*Courage to be who you are long enough to change perceptions*

**Chapter 6:** The Stare                                                     35

*The drive of a leader*

**Chapter 7:** OK, Now This      39
*Open-mindedness*

**Chapter 8:** Catching the Fast Dog at the Park      45
*Compete where you naturally excel*

**Chapter 9:** Zeke, Inc.      49
*Create and nurture a personal brand*

**Chapter 10:** Shoe Leather      53
*Developing personal resilience*

**Chapter 11:** Get the Cookie, Paco!      59
*Turning neuroticism into determination*

**Chapter 12:** One Mood, All the Time      65
*Emotional intelligence and self-awareness*

**Chapter 13:** "Zeke, Quit Licking Your Foot!"      71
*Changing tactics as the situation changes*


**II. WORKING WITH OTHERS**      77

**Chapter 14:** Forget Beer–Dogs are the Real Social Lubricant      79
*Directing and aligning the efforts of others*

**Chapter 15:** To Adopt or Not?      91
*Learning how in-groups and out-groups work*

**Chapter 16:** Facebook for Dogs      97
*Building a network your own way*

**Chapter 17:** Following Like a Lost Puppy      103
*The importance of a first follower*

**Chapter 18:** The Dog Park Ambassador      109
*Relationship building*

**Chapter 19:** Bad Dog!      115
*Using negative feedback to your advantage*

**Chapter 20:** Owners are Friends with Money      121
*The importance of resources and contacts*

**Chapter 21:** Quietly the Best                                      125
*Balancing self-confidence with humility*
**Chapter 22:** Puppy Dog Eyes                                        129
*Developing personal magnetism*
**Chapter 23:** Treats or Shouts                                      133
*Fear-based leading versus love-based leading*

**III. READING OTHERS**                                               139
**Chapter 24:** "Blah Blah Hungry, Zeke?"                             141
*Sort through the fluff to get to the main message*
**Chapter 25:** Paco See, Paco Do                                     147
*Matching your actions, tone, and mood to connect with others*
**Chapter 26:** Getting Past "Woof"                                   153
*Nonverbal communication is still communication*
**Chapter 27:** Babbling to Babies and Dogs                           159
*Conversation is an art*
**Chapter 28:** Whimpering in Your Blanket                            165
*Recognizing the complexity in others*

**IV. LEADING OTHERS**                                                169
**Chapter 29:** Not Always the Top Dog                                171
*When to lead and when to follow*
**Chapter 30:** How Old is He… She?                                   175
*Gender and leadership ability*
**Chapter 31:** Wanna Go to the Beach?                                179
*Using emotion-provoking words*
**Chapter 32:** What a Dog Wants                                      183
*Thinking strategically*
**Chapter 33:** Play-dar                                              187
*People like those who like them*

**Chapter 34:** Looking Guilty Together     193
*Taking one for the team*

**Chapter 35:** When to Jump on the Couch     197
*Reading and responding to the emotional element*

**Chapter 36:** Twenty Steps in Advance     203
*Leading at just the right distance*

**Chapter 37:** Who is Walking Whom?     209
*Influence works in any direction*

**Chapter 38:** Dog's Dependence     213
*Accruing power*

**Chapter 39:** "Wait" Doesn't mean "Stop"     219
*Communicating with clarity and consistency*

**Chapter 40:** Answers Without Questions     225
Balancing theory and practice


**V. THE BIGGER PICTURE**     **229**

**Chapter 41:** The Canoe     231
*Leading your life with a light touch*

**Chapter 42:** The Power of Presence     235
*Raising awareness by just being there*

**Chapter 43:** You Can't Use Shock Collars in the Office     241
*Leadership versus dominance*

**Chapter 44:** The Richest Dog Doesn't Have a Dime     245
*Wisdom and grace as measures of wealth*

**Chapter 45:** Paco Now Eats Carrots     251
*Chasing other people's desires is a waste of time*

**Chapter 46:** Chewing Gum Saves Lives     257
*Creating space in the midst of panic and hurry*

**Chapter 47:** Hooray for the Packaging     263
*Finding value in the mundane*

**Chapter 48:** Finger at the Moon                                                  267
*Looking past what is said to what is meant*
**Chapter 49:** We Don't All Need to be Show Dogs                      273
*The perils of being too professional*
**Chapter 50:** Animal Altruism                                                   279
*Bringing together natural enemies*
**Chapter 51:** Gain Power by Giving it Away                              283
*Power is not a finite resource*
**Chapter 52:** Snap Out of It and Go Throw a Ball                     287
*Help people look beyond self-interest*


**VI. PARTING THOUGHTS**                                                        **291**


Epilogue                                                                                295
About the Author                                                                     299
Bibliography                                                                          301

**Paco and Zeke on the dunes of Cape Cod**

All knowledge, the totality of all questions
and answers, is contained in the dog.
—Franz Kafka, Investigations of the Dog

*For my beautiful wife, Michaele, my partner in all these adventures,*

*and of course for Zeke and Paco*

# Acknowledgments

Like any endeavor in life, this book came into existence through the influence and help of many people.

It certainly couldn't have happened if my wife, Michaele, hadn't brought her spindly little spider monkey of a puppy into my life, or if her parents, Kathy and Jon, hadn't opened their hearts and home to two little stray dogs (Paco and his brother Pancho) a few months earlier. Michaele's ongoing moral support and encouragement on the book project (and her amazing vegetarian cooking) have been instrumental to its successful completion. I want to also thank my parents Sarah and Olaf for bringing me up in a world of books and learning, where practically every fourth wall in every room in the house consisted of a full bookcase (except maybe the kitchen and bathroom). They instilled the love of the written word in me from when I was just a "pup."

A thank you goes to Joe Mistich, who urged me for years to "Write a book!" His unwavering faith in me provided the impetus to begin. Thanks also goes to Dr. Anne Randerson, who undertook the unenviable task of editing the first version of the book through our directed study work together, and to Melissa Rancourt for her enthusiasm and faith in me as I navigated the steps of plotting my own entrepreneurial path.

I would also like to thank Dr. Matthieu Raillard, my old friend and Colgate roommate, for inspiring me to write a book a dozen years ago when he wrote his first novel in the midst of our senior year final exams. His amnesiac assassin hero is the philosopher's Jason Bourne.

Finally, I want to acknowledge the continued good work and selflessness of the countless individuals working in and with animal shelters across the country and those who choose to adopt from them. These professionals provide the rest of us the chance to do one of the few truly noble things in life—to save another life.

# Introduction

My wife and I met at a dog park in New Orleans a few months before Hurricane Katrina. On a warm, wet May day, I took my nine-month-old rescued mutt, Zeke, down to Coliseum Square.

The park, an unofficial leash-free zone in the neighborhood, was empty since few dog owners enjoy cleaning up the mess that results from playing in the grass after a subtropical downpour. Within a few minutes two cute girls showed up with a blue heeler puppy named Paco. He was a bit shy and mostly hid behind one of the girl's legs, while Zeke, in all his foolish glory, ran laps around the park and spun like an alligator in the mud. The girls and I struck up a conversation about how ridiculously our animals were behaving.

The next morning on my way out of the local coffee shop with a French roast in my hand, I spotted Paco and one of the girls. I wracked my brain but could not remember either of the girls' names, so on my way past, I said hello and made sure to call Paco by his name. Over the next two months I headed down to the park every day after work, hoping to catch him and his cute owner again. It turns out Michaele was trying to coordinate her visits to see me as well. We would wait for each other down by the fountain, each playing it cool when the other showed up. After a few weeks we started dating in earnest, and I learned more about her and about how she ended up with Paco.

A few months earlier Michaele's parents had been visiting a friend at his ranch outside of Houston. Her mother had found two stray puppies who looked not more than a few weeks old. Apparently they had wandered away from their mother on a neighboring property. When the owner of the other property was approached about them, he shrugged and said, "I guess the coyotes will get them." Of course, my future mother-in-law couldn't bear the thought of that and brought them back to her home north of New Orleans. She named the grey one Paco and the black one Pancho. Michaele took one look at Paco and knew he had to be hers. She took him with her as she moved into her new apartment on Camp Street, next to the park.

Two months after I met them that soggy day at the park, Hurricane Katrina hit. Like everyone else in the area, we were forced to evacuate our homes and our city. I ended up with Michaele's family in Houston for a few weeks as a temporary solution, until it was clear that no one was returning to New Orleans for a while. I had one semester of business school left at Tulane University, and I needed to make some decisions regarding school. I contacted the dean of UC Davis, who agreed to let me finish my studies in her program. Soon I was on my way to California. It did not take long for Michaele to decide to join me on this adventure. We packed up my little Acura with the dogs, a cooler of food, and our few salvaged bags. Then we started driving west.

Since then the four of us have been all over the place. We have lived in several places on the West Coast, in the Gulf South, New England, and most recently in Brussels, Belgium. The dogs, now six and five years old, have dipped their paws in the Pacific Ocean, the Gulf of Mexico, the Atlantic Ocean, and the North Sea. We joke that they're two of the most well-traveled pets in the world. Who else has seen so much of the world at only five years old?

They have adapted well to all of the relocations, and each time they provide an immediate sense of home, which helps us acclimate. Home is where the dog is.

But this book isn't about the generic benefits of owning a dog or what kinds of joy (or stress) they can provide. This book came into being because I realized that our two dogs—each very distinct from the other in personality—are constantly teaching us lessons on everyday leadership.

The concept of leadership has been gaining popularity in recent years. In business school it was a required course, even though many of my hardened classmates felt it was "too soft" to be of any use. I disagreed then, and I still do.

In my ensuing years as a consultant, I witnessed how business owners and employees completely ignored the *human* element of business—the fact that emotions rule decision making. There is a pervasive assumption that if you have the technical answer to a problem, it should be solved. They believe that as long as you know what should be done, then people should fall in line. How wrong this is.

This is true both in and out of the office. Many people are kept back from their potential because they haven't been taught—or simply don't consider—what it is to be a leader and how to become one. They don't know how to effectively implement change through motivating others. As one client told me, "The problem with business is that you have to deal with *people*." And that's messy. It struck me that most people couldn't imagine themselves as leaders. The role to them is mysterious and opaque, a peak in the distance with no path up. It's viewed as an all-or-nothing condition, that there are leaders and followers, but nothing in between. I disagree. The more I work with the concept of leadership, the more I realize that it's like climbing a mountain: there are easy ways up and difficult ones. Some people are in better shape than others. Guidance, either in the form of a map, GPS, or skilled guide, always helps. Not everyone is going to reach the summit, but with a little effort they can climb a bit higher and enjoy the view.

# Get the Cookie, Paco!

I decided I was going to be that skilled guide. I enrolled in the graduate-level leadership program offered at Boston University's Brussels campus. One day, well into my first semester, I was studying for the next day's class and Paco and Zeke were pacing around, bored.[1] I went to the kitchen and got two rawhide bones—a.k.a. "cookies"—to occupy them for a while. I instructed them to sit and then handed over the cookies. Zeke snatched his and immediately plopped on the floor and started chewing away with his muscular jaws. Paco, on the other hand, brought the cookie to the middle of the room, spat it out, and then proceeded to yip and dance around it just like a puppy. He snuck up on it as if it were a snake. Then he nosed it and jumped back and spun his head around in a playful manner. Next he ran up to the cookie, grabbed it, and tossed his head. He sent the cookie flying into the other room and quickly skidded off to do the whole routine all over again.

This went on for five minutes or so, during which time Zeke had diligently chewed through half his bone. Finally Paco got bored since I wasn't joining in on the fun. He came up and stared at me like he didn't know what to do next. I had to tell him, "Get the cookie, Paco! Go get it!" over and over before he finally tired of making a show of it and settled in to chewing. To Paco, it's all a big game and it's always the same, whether it's the first cookie of the day or the third.

All at once it hit me. The way each dog had reacted to his cookie was just like the way different clients of mine had approached certain tasks they had to accomplish. Some settled in immediately to get the work done, focused on the task. They finished quickly and without fanfare. Others put off completing the task, got distracted, made a show of it, and created drama or side issues that delayed the completion of the task. These clients were more interested in being recognized by others for the work they were doing, or they used the task as a way to bring up other unrelated issues and unproductive distractions. They needed to be gently told to focus on completing the task itself. How many times had I essentially encouraged clients to stop playing around and "Get the cookie?"

[1] City life can be tough for a dog. There's so much happening outside the door and they spend hours sitting in a small apartment waiting for the chance to explore it. At least in the country they don't feel like they are missing as much.

I realized that the dogs had illustrated a key lesson in leadership. A leader needs to be able to focus on the important tasks at hand and not get too caught up in side distractions. Using assignments as political tools for attention can be harmful to the organization and demoralizing to others. As the months went on, I took mental notes when my experience with the dogs illustrated key lessons covered in my leadership curriculum.

I wrote this book to pass those lessons on to you. There's a tendency to think that being a leader is harder than it actually is. People tend to think: *If I can't become a leader like Mother Theresa or George Washington, then why even try?* When most people think of leadership, they don't think of those small and noticeable actions that they can take every day to improve themselves and their effectiveness with other people. They tend to think about how far they are from the leadership role models they admire, and they get overwhelmed or frustrated with the difference they perceive. Others tend to dismiss leadership as not relevant to them.

If you interact with people on a daily basis, then you will benefit from these lessons. Leadership isn't just for politicians and CEOs to study. It's for stay-at-home parents, bookstore clerks, and students too.

We need leaders now more than ever. Our world is becoming more complex daily, creating new challenges for leaders. No matter what side of the political spectrum you're on, we need to do more than just look to others for guidance. We need to become the guides ourselves, little by little. The problems we face as we head further in to the twenty-first century need collective effort, where we stand up and take action to solve them. Simply sitting back and assuming others will fix our problems doesn't work.[2] If we all increase our everyday leadership skills, even just a little, the accumulated result will be outstanding.

So how do we all become better leaders? The more I studied leadership, the more it seemed that any advice on the subject seemed to fall into two

---

[2] If you doubt this, go browse the books in the current affairs or politics section of your local bookstore.

categories: too simple to be meaningful or too complex to be useful. On one side was the inspirational coffee mug proclaiming *Leaders Create Excellence for Everybody!* and on the other is the journal article entitled "Toward an Adequate Taxonomy of Personality Attributes: Replicated Factor Structure in Peer Nomination Personality Ratings" (which, by the way, is a real journal article). My feelings were echoed in an excellent textbook[3] that lamented that most leadership practitioners either preach case studies (too academic and dry) or maxims (too "one size fits all"). They conclude that "leadership researchers need to do a better job of making the findings from their studies more relevant and accessible to practicing managers and leaders."

For that reason, I hope this book lands in the sweet spot between "easy and useless" and "academic and dry." We'll be looking at findings from the decades of leadership study, but we'll also be considering what they might mean to us in everyday situations. Leadership is an active concept, not a static one. We become leaders by our actions more than our thoughts. I'm reminded of the advice Dr. Leo Marvin (played by Richard Dreyfuss) gives to his patient Bob Wiley (played by Bill Murray) in the movie *What About Bob?*: "Take baby steps." Taking this to heart, Bob walks out of the therapy session staring at his feet while shuffling with little steps and mumbling the mantra, "Baby steps out the door, baby steps down the hall, baby steps into the elevator..." This is what I hope you do with the lessons in this book. Read them. See which ones resonate with you. Try them out. Take baby steps down the hall, out the door, and all the way to becoming a better leader.

I want to stress that these are lessons in *everyday* leadership. The lessons are easy—so easy that my dogs know them instinctively. There are opportunities for all of us to apply these lessons as we go about our day. Many of these aren't difficult and do not require much effort. Apply these lessons to your life, and you will see a slow but measurably positive outcome. They may not get you a promotion tomorrow, but they will make you more effective in living the kind of life you want to live.

---

[3] Hughes, Ginnett and Curphy 2009

Many of the chapters in this book cover topics that will be very familiar to you—for instance, the importance of persistence and of charisma, focusing on your goals, and developing emotional intelligence. My aim is not to rehash these well-established topics, but rather to give you another perspective on them through the antics of my dogs. Sometimes all it takes is one new perspective on an old theme to finally have an aha! moment. If nothing else, the chapters should provide some amusement to those of us who are continually entertained by our pets.

Each of the short chapters uses a true story about Paco and Zeke to get the lesson across. Some begin with the dogs; others begin with a concept in leadership. The chapters fall under five sections: Working on Yourself, Working with Others, Reading Others, Leading Others, and The Bigger Picture. You may either read the book straight through or jump around from chapter to chapter. Each lesson is self-contained, and there are fifty-two in the book. Paco and Zeke continue to teach me a few more every month. For all of you who already have a dog, this book may help you to see them in a new light.

Buddhists talk about a "diamond under your feet." This means that there is something very valuable already right there next to you that you just haven't seen or recognized yet. Now that I see the lessons that we can learn from our dogs if we just pay attention, I think I know what they mean.

Andrew Kruger

Brussels

July 2010

# I

# Working on Yourself

There are several reasons why you may want to work on yourself. The first and most obvious is that you may want to learn what traits are associated with successful leaders and begin to adopt them for yourself. Another reason may be that you're aware that the best place to start is internally, by growing down. "Growing down shifts the focus of the personality from...single minded egocentricity...into common humanity, twisting the call to transcend toward extension into the world and its claims." [4]

In other words, if you want to get what's *out there,* you need to start *in here.*

This section contains lessons on how to look inside and work with what you have. Since self-knowledge is the foundation of true wisdom and improvement, it made sense to put this section first. We'll take a look at fear

---

[4] Clements and Washbush 1999

of action, fear of constraints, and the fear of seeing things as they really are. We'll discuss knowing when to persevere and when to quit, and how to keep a steady and open mind ready to accept change.

In addition we'll consider why Paco can't swim, why Zeke has the biggest image problems (but solves them by simply not caring), and why Paco's stare is one of his biggest assets.

# 1

# Just Jump In
*Acting without complete information*

On hot days in California we took the dogs swimming in the inland lakes. We'd pack up for a day trip, drive through the wine country, and find a little spot to park the car and cool off in the water. As with most lakes in the area, there wasn't really a beach but more of a grassy area that led to a foot-high drop into the water. As my wife and I would wade in, Zeke would just plunge right in and start paddling around. We'd make it out into the deeper area past where we could touch the ground, and Zeke would be swimming around us merrily, looking for a stick or some toy to retrieve. Paco, on the other hand, would stay right at the edge of the shore, clearly annoyed that he was left behind, and just start barking at us. As a herding dog, he's happiest when everyone is in a group formation—cattle, sheep, people, it doesn't matter. By wading out we clearly had broken up the group, and he let us know.

"Well, come on out then!" we'd call to him, which only incited him to yip more desperately. I'd head back to shore and try to coax him in the water, but he would not have any of it. He'd avoid my reach or plant his little paws in the dirt. If I did manage to catch him and lead him a little into the water, he'd follow nervously as long as his paws could touch. But once he got out to the point where his belly hit the water, he'd try to climb *on top* of the water. Since he could see there was a surface, he thought, *I should just be able to climb up on that surface.* The result was hilarious. He would end up with his head directly over his submerged tail, and he'd smack his front paws on the water to try to pull himself up. At the same time he'd point his nose straight up in the air to avoid splashing himself in the face. It never worked. He never could figure out the water.

As I saw it, the problem was that Paco was thinking about it too much. Zeke was a little less of a cerebral dog, so he just jumped in and figured it out. He may have splashed around a bit the first few minutes the first time he tried it, but he quickly learned on the fly and was swimming in no time. In fact, with his short hair, muscular body, and big round head he looked just like one of those seals you see on the docks at Fisherman's Wharf in San Francisco. To be fair, Paco is an Australian cattle dog and probably doesn't have the swimming gene in his blood. But he overanalyzed how to approach the water, and therefore he never learned how to swim. He could never join us in the water.

We have all experienced times when something seems impossible to tackle because we just can't figure out how to go about it. The clearest memory of it for me involved book reports back in grade school. I remember reading the book and sitting down at the computer glumly, staring at the blank page in front of me. *How do I begin this thing?* Although there were guidelines I was supposed to follow, there was no one right way to start it. The older we get, the fewer guidelines there tend to be. The places that have the strictest rules on how to accomplish a task tend to be the ones that stifle us, bore us, or make us feel as if we are suffocating.

For a while after college I worked for a large cell phone company doing collections work. I was the guy who called you when you didn't pay your bill for several months. It was all strictly regulated: the way we were supposed to make a call, what we were supposed to say, and how we were supposed to say it. We even were given scripts of exactly, word for word, what to say to a customer who had not paid his bill. I didn't last too long there as I felt too stifled. I also felt that this "one size fits all" approach did not allow me to work with each person as an individual for the best outcome. As I got into more interesting work, though, the more freedom I had to accomplish the tasks in the way I saw fit. I was held accountable for the results of the work I did, not the path I took to get there.

These are the times that leadership comes into play. Leaders push past what is already established and chart a new path. If they are lucky, they may have some rough idea of how to move forward but often they do not. The lesson from the dogs is to not overthink or overstrategize how to begin. At some point you have to jump in with imperfect knowledge and just figure out the rest as you go along. I believe Jack Welsh is quoted as saying, "A leader is the one acting on 75 percent complete information." If he waits until the information is 95 percent complete, he would be a follower.

Some of us, especially those of us who consistently push ourselves and aspire to improve, tend to rely heavily on strategy before action. Of course it is wise to learn what you can and devise an approach to tackle an issue or chart a course of action, but at some point you have to put the map down and start driving down the actual road. Often we have less time to prepare than what we'd like. There's the presentation to give next week at work or the family dilemma that arises at the last minute and has to be resolved.

My wife read that when blue heelers are herding they will run across the top of the backs of a group of animals just to get to the straying animal on the other side of the pack the fastest. When you think about it, this is an amazing adaptation. At some point the dogs broke free from the traditional routes to the other side of the pack—go around to the left or go around to the right—and realized that there was another more attractive option: *What if I just go over the top?* This dog was bred to strategize each move for the most beneficial results. It's funny to think that water, one of the simplest and most ubiquitous aspects of living, has confounded him.

There is one situation, however, where the roles are reversed and Zeke is the hesitant one and Paco just goes for it: treats. From the time he was a puppy, Zeke had sensitive skin and was prone to periodic rashes. Some even got infected and required rounds of antibiotics, for which I had the undesirable task of trying to get him to take a pill twice a day for a week or more. There are only so many ways that you can hide a pill in food before the dog finds out what you are doing. After I successfully hid the pill in bread a few times, he figured out what I was doing and refused to eat it. Next I tried peanut butter, again with limited success. He would chew up the peanut butter and spit out the pill. All of these tricks made him very suspicious of any food that wasn't delivered in a bowl. Now, years later, if I call the dogs over and tell them I have a treat for them, Zeke acts as if all offerings are potential poison[5]. I'll toss a treat to Paco, who will rise up on his back legs to snatch it out of the air, but if I toss one to Zeke, he will let it bounce off his nose and then eye it suspiciously once it hits the ground. Of course, it only lasts a second on the ground before Paco snaps that one up as well.

It's not that we don't hide pills in Paco's food too. He just doesn't care. The payoff of getting the treat is worth the slim risk of any hidden medicine. But Zeke, who lets a few negative experiences color his current perception of treats, misses out on getting most treats by being too suspicious and taking too long to act.

---

[5] As I noted in the introduction, Zeke is quick to grab a rawhide "cookie" because he knows that I can't hide a pill in it. However, any other form of treat or edible is treated with grave suspicion.

There are times when overthinking not only keeps us from advancing, but it can also lead us into worse situations than the one we started out in. For my birthday a few years back, we went camping north of San Francisco by the Russian River. We rented inflatable canoes that would hold two people and two dogs, and we planned on spending the day lazily floating down the river. Getting the dogs in the canoe was challenging enough, but once we had pushed off and started paddling to the middle of the river, Paco flipped out. He somehow decided that since he was around water (but not in it), the water posed a threat, and he jumped out of the canoe and started splashing his way toward the shore. My wife jumped out after him and was able to walk on the riverbed as the water was only about four feet deep. Paco, of course, was splashing around in circles with his head straight up in the air but somehow drifting closer to his intended destination, the shore.

Lining this section of the shore was about a three-foot-high patch of reeds. Paco headed right for them as Michaele tried to catch up to him. He got there first. His thrashing twisted him around in the reeds, and it looked like he was being devoured by some creature with a thousand tentacles. While he was never in any real danger, getting all four of his feet tangled in the reeds while he was still technically over his head in the water was not his idea of a good time. After Michaele extracted him (she was thanked with a patchwork of scratches from his flailing claws), he bounded on to the shore wide-eyed and spent the rest of the day running alongside us safely from the shore.

Zeke, meanwhile, was contentedly sitting in the canoe, watching the drama unfold. If he could have popped open a beer and munched on some Cheetos, he would have. In his stress and overthinking the danger he was in, Paco had created three undesirable outcomes for himself. First, he made his fears come true by choosing to jump out of the canoe. Second, he immediately got himself into a worse situation by getting tangled in the reeds. And third, he ended up spending the day separated from the group and having to run alongside us rather than enjoying a leisurely float down the river.

This "out of the frying pan into the fire" meme is common in entertainment too. How many times have we seen a character on a sitcom take a situation, stress about possible negative consequences, and then work themselves into an even worse situation than the original one? This theme is so often used that we may not see that it actually happens to us as well. Next time you are confronted with a difficult situation or some task that seems insurmountable, know when to stop thinking about it and strategizing, and when to jump in with the knowledge you have and just give it your best effort, learning as you go.

Leaders gather information, but know that at some point you have to take what you have, whether you like it or not, and just act on it. Being a leader often means being in situations that are not clearly defined. These are the situations where most people are afraid to act. Leaders take what they know and just jump in when the situation demands it.

# Lesson

Sometimes the solution is not as complex as you think, and the solution is best found by just jumping in and giving it your best shot. It helps to have a strategy, but it is important to know when to move from thinking about the strategy to implementing it, even if you feel like you have incomplete information.

# 2

Fighting the Leash

*Knowing when to leave well enough alone*


When we lived out in San Francisco, we used to take weekend road trips whenever we could. We used to laugh at how everyone said, "Oh, the Bay Area is the best! We have the mountains an hour away, the beach right here, and freshwater lakes and Napa Valley vineyards are only a short drive away!" Well, it turns out they were right. Any morning you woke up restless (and didn't have to work) you could hop in the car and take off to explore.

One weekend we chose to go on a four-wheeler tour around the outskirts of Yosemite State Park. The dogs—of course—came with us. We had joined in with another couple, and the four of us hired a tour guide to take us—via four-wheeler—deep into the mountains. As the tour did not really work with the dogs (we imagined Paco trying to herd the four-wheelers into a little group, and Zeke giving up and lying down in the trail fifteen minutes in), they stayed in the car. What we typically did on nice days was to open the back hatch of the Subaru and attach the leashes to the little metal cargo tie-downs in the back of the car. This way the dogs could hop in and out as needed, resting in the back of the car or sniffing around in the dirt. And any urges to relieve themselves would at least have an option to be completed outside the car.

Upon arrival at the guide's house, we parked the car and set the dogs up. The car was parked off to the side of the yard, out of the way of any other moving vehicles. It was a perfect day—seventy-two degrees and calm, with the sun peeking through the high tree cover in the area. We popped open the hatch and the dogs shot out to explore their new surroundings as we set the leashes up. One was tied to a metal loop over the left wheel well, the other to a loop on the right. Each leash was about seven feet long, enough for the dogs to move around comfortably. We called them over and hooked them up—always red leash for Paco, blue for Zeke[6]. Then we headed in with our friends to meet our guide.

We weren't a hundred feet away, by the front door, before Paco started yipping and yelping in his characteristic ear-splitting tone. I walked back toward the car to find the dogs tied in a knot. The leashes wove around each other in a tight and contorted way, and the dogs were tangled up against each other, each with about five inches of play in their leash between the knot and their collars. As I walked up, they got more frenetic in anticipation of being freed from their newly created binds. They squirmed and yipped, their heads and bodies pulling apart momentarily before crashing into each other again, getting more and more entangled.

---

[6] This is for my sake, not theirs. Paco chews and salivates all over his leash, so it builds up a stiff crustiness over time. I'd rather limit that nastiness to just one leash.

In less than two minutes, Paco and Zeke had taken a pleasant situation for themselves and literally tied themselves in a knot. While it's true that they started off with limitations, each being on a leash only so long, they complicated and made their situation worse by freaking out and fighting the leash. Twisting and turning, pulling and tangling, they reduced their freedom by about 90 percent almost immediately.

I unhitched them from their leashes and unwove the knot. "Let's try that again," I told them as I reattached them in their original positions. I stood a few feet away behind the car, just out of their reach but in full sight. They stood alert and happy, wagging their tales and looking at me expectantly. I waited a few minutes, watching them relax a bit. Then I stepped out of sight to test them.

In no time came the yelping again. It was clear that the only way to resolve this—and return to my patient wife and friends—was to keep them in the car with all the windows down. They would be in the cool shade, and the dog grate installed behind the rear seats would keep them from hopping out any of the open windows. They would be safe and comfortable, but now they had to spend the next few hours staring out of the smudged windows looking for squirrels. They had succeeded in being leash free but were now contained.

The lesson here is that if you find yourself under new constraints, take the time to evaluate your situation calmly before simply losing it and fighting what you perceive to be a bad situation. Remaining calm in pressure situations is a key trait of leaders. The ability to adjust to new constraints and to consider them from a larger perspective is important. Leaders identify which aspects of the new situation they have to fight and which ones they can work with to meet existing objectives and goals.

Had the dogs been able to realize that being on the leash meant being able to be outside of the car, enjoying the breeze and barking at the rustling leaves, maybe they would not have fought it so hard. Yes, it was more restrictive than being able to run free, but it was better than being completely contained in the back of the car.

Many people encounter situations that seem restricting, and they fight violently and adamantly, only to find their new circumstances much more restrictive. Consider the teenager who thinks that an 11:00 p.m. curfew is too early and stays out until 2:00 a.m. in protest. Not only does he prove that he's not responsible enough to handle the 11:00 p.m. curfew, but he almost guarantees that future curfews are much earlier—that is, if he's allowed to go out at all. Or consider the employee who feels that a new procedure to punch a timecard does not apply to her, as she feels it is unfair and more restrictive than the old method of merely writing her daily hours down. The employee may fight the procedure, continuing to write her hours on the card and not use the time clock to officially punch the card. Come payday, she might not have a paycheck at all since she did not use the correct procedure. "Fighting the leash" for the teenager and the employee in these examples did not help them out at all; in fact it brought them to a more restrictive place.

Other times, of course, fighting the leash is worth it. Sometimes constraints really are unfair and should be reduced or overcome. The key is taking the right approach. Imagine if the teen in our example above sat down with his parents and explained that an 11:00 p.m. curfew is too early, but he understands why they want to ensure he's safe. He proposes calling them at 11:00 p.m. to let them know how and where is, promising to be home by midnight. Using this approach he may actually get the curfew pushed back permanently. Or consider if the employee asked to speak with her manager, explaining that some of the employees see the new use of timecards as mistrust from management. She may try to get to the root of the problem with management by showing them she's on their side and pointing out the potential negative unintended consequences of the new policy. There is no guarantee that the policy will be reversed, but this approach produces better results in the long run.

# Lesson

If you are suddenly facing new constraints, tied up with only a little room to move, and you struggle to free yourself without giving the situation some calm thought first, you may just make things worse. It can get even more restricting if there is someone else who is tied up with you as well.

# 3

## "Don't Worry, We're Coming Right Back!"

### *Keeping your mind in the now*

I'm a fan of Eastern philosophy. After having delved into Taoism in college, I spent about a decade reading about Buddhism. One of the central themes—which exists in some form in every religion—is the importance of being in the moment. Eckhart Tolle, who wrote the excellent book *The Power of Now*, commented that he has met many Zen masters, all of them cats. I'd argue that dogs, while not quite at the level of cats, also have an uncanny ability to be fully present right now and not too concerned with past or future concerns.

The most obvious example of this is when we leave the dogs alone so that we can run an errand. Zeke and Paco get very depressed when we walk out the door. They are truly living only in that moment as they are being left alone and don't appear to take any solace in the fact that we always come back. As soon as we return through the door, of course, it may as well be the stroke of midnight on New Year's Eve—lots of fanfare, excitement, and joy. Paco yips and runs in circles, and Zeke rears up awkwardly on his little hind legs, top-heavy but wild-eyed and giddy. And this is just when we take a five minute trip to the post office.

Of course my own path to living in the now has not been quite so direct. Like most people, my natural childhood ability to experience the joy of the moment became gradually replaced with social and educational formalities. My relationship with meditation—one of the most successful methods to living in the now—has been fitful. At first I delved in and dedicated ten minutes every morning to it. I would slip out of bed, onto my red mediation cushion, and sit. My most successful technique was counting to ten. It sounded so simple. I would try counting to ten slowly, one number per breath, watching to see if I was interrupted by thought. It usually went like this: "One...two...*boy it's cold here this morning. I wonder if I should put on a sweater...Argh, a thought! OK now, begin again.* One...two...three...*what is that spot on the wall? Was that there yesterday? Argh!* One...*why is it so hard to meditate this morning? Argh!* One..."

It seems like such a simple thing: just sit. But it isn't. Somehow I could find hours to waste on YouTube but couldn't find ten minutes to sit. Nevertheless I always return to meditation. One of my best reminders to return to the zafu[7] is a postcard I found in a local bookstore in Madison, Wisconsin, years ago. On it was a quote by Franz Kafka:

> You do not need to leave your room. Remain sitting at
> your table and listen. Do not even listen, simply wait. Do

---

[7] Mediation cushion

not even wait; be quite still and solitary. The world will
freely offer itself to you to be unmasked; it has no choice.
It will roll in ecstasy at your feet.[8]

It was brilliant and became etched somewhere in the back of my head.
With this ever-present reminder, how could I stop trying to meditate?
Now the dogs help me to stay motivated. Every day I see Paco "rolling in
ecstasy" in tune with the joyous world he lives in. Every morning he bursts
with love of life, as if sleep for him was a little death that he wasn't ever
sure he'd come back from. Of course he still experiences bad times (like
every time he's left alone); he just enjoys the good in the full vividness of
the moment.

Thanks to his bloodline, however, Paco does frequently slip into worry
and anticipation. It usually works like this: He's on the floor, happily lost in
the moment of chewing on a toy, not a care in the world. Life is perfect. Then
he hears the clarion call of my keys jingling as I swipe them from the counter. His head shoots up. *Is he going outside? Wait...am I going outside?* Now his
little beady herding dog eyes are transfixed on me. I can practically feel his
stare. *He's going toward my leash! We're going outside! Yay!* He's no longer in the
moment. Now he's anticipating our walk. And he's no longer happy. Now he's
*squeathing.*[9] If we don't go out in the next ten seconds, he is an agony. *Why
aren't we outside yet?* His world has fallen apart.

Leadership is about strategy, planning, and thinking. But it's also about
being in the moment. The leader who knows herself, and is comfortable in
her own skin and quiet mind, is at a tremendous advantage. With this still
yet mindful awareness she can more efficiently assess and respond to the
environment.

---

[8] Kafka 1961
[9] We've coined this term to describe the unique (and annoying) sound Paco can make when he's
simultaneously squeaking and breathing. Every exhale creates a high-pitched whine.

Better yet, she is responding to what is *actually* happening and not her knee-jerk mental models[10] further clouded by incessant internal chatter.[11]

The leader who is better able to live in the moment has improved understanding of himself. He has better self-regulation, which means that he can recognize and work with his own emotions as situations arise. He is less likely to lose himself and his emotions in stressful situations. Therefore, his responses to them will be more appropriate and not purely emotional. Self-regulation is one component of emotional intelligence, which has been long recognized as a characteristic of high-quality leaders.

---

[10] More on mental models in chapter 7, "OK, Now This."
[11] Will Sparks referred to this accurately as the "news ticker." Just like that little bar at the bottom of your favorite twenty-four-hour news channel, we all have a non-stop mental commentary that just keeps running and running and running...

# Lesson

Learn to live in the moment. Take up meditation. Be "quite still and solitary" for a few minutes each day, every day. Then increase those few minutes to twenty minutes. What you gain in personal awareness, contentment, and perspective will astound you. You'll then start to bring each of those qualities into your interactions with others, which will make them respond to you in positive ways. Your charisma, influence, and emotional intelligence—all characteristics of great leaders—will begin to flourish.

# 4

## Being Bulldogged
### *Persistence*

When leadership scholars began to look for effective personal leadership traits in the early twentieth century, they lumped them all under five general categories:

1. Capacity (intelligence, alertness, verbal facility, originality, judgment)

2. Achievement (scholarship, knowledge, athletic accomplishments)

3. Responsibility (dependability, initiative, persistence, aggressiveness, self-confidence, desire to excel)

4. Participation (activity, sociability, cooperation, adaptability, humor)

5. Status (socioeconomic position, popularity)[12]

In this chapter, we look more closely at responsibility, in particular the assertive traits of initiative, persistence, aggressiveness, and self-confidence.

Much has been written about persistence in going after what you want. We've all been told that anything worth having is worth waiting for, or worth working for. I have always considered myself determined. That is, until I understood why a synonym for determined is *bulldogged.*

When we take the dogs out for a walk, I usually end up walking Zeke. Now this may have something to do with the fact that he was the dog I brought to the relationship, so he can be thought of as "my dog." (Usually that label only applies when he did something wrong, as in when Michaele asks, "Can you believe that *your dog* tore into the fifty-pound food bag and ate a quarter of it?") However, the real reason why I tend to walk him is that I offer more pulling power to counteract his. This dog, when he wants to, can become *immobile.* It's almost as if he bolts himself to the ground at will.

Now it's not a question of mass, because I'm easily two-and-a-half times his weight. He uses some canine-ninja technique that we haven't exactly figured out yet. It usually works like this: we are out for a pleasant walk and Zeke is on the leash trailing a step or two behind as usual. All of a sudden he will stop dead in his tracks. I don't notice and continue at my risk pace, until the leash gets tight and pulls my arm sharply back, popping shoulder ligaments I didn't know I had. Zeke hunches down in his ninja position, head down and looking up at me with a steely stare, all four paws planted firmly against any forward movement. Why? It could be for any number of reasons. A sign post he wants to smell. A discarded fast food bag. Or no apparent reason at all. He just wants to...stop. Right. Now.

---

[12] This entire list is from Stogdill 1948

It's on—a battle of wills. I grumble, "Come *on,* Zeke!" and give a tug. He leans back against the leash, rolls of skin bunching up from his neck, making him look like a shar-pei momentarily. I pull with all of my weight, and his nails start skidding forward and he relents, trotting forward. I've won for now. We used to fight this battle a few times a day, especially when there was no clear reason why he wants to stop, but lately he's worn me down with his persistence.

Zeke knows that he's the only one who wants to stop. It's one against four—those are tough odds. But statistics isn't one of his talents.[13] At the beginning his success rate was about 10 percent, but these days I put up much less resistance and give him his extended sniffing time about 60 percent of the time.

To me, this exhibited the pure power of persistence. There were no other factors at play—no arguments, persuasions, or reasons why he needed to stop. There was just unadulterated will to achieve his goal. And he eventually got his way.

The evidence shows that when it comes to leader effectiveness, personal traits do matter. Chief among them are those related to drive. One study found that "leaders are more likely than non-leaders to have a high level of energy and stamina and be generally active, lively, and often restless."[14] In addition they have a "degree of strength of will or perseverance"[15] and "must be tirelessly persistent in their activities and follow through with their programs."[16] At times the dogs join forces to wear us down. When they want to get fed, or we are taking too long over coffee in the morning and they want to get to the park, they weave back and forth between us, first one, then the other, trying to get us going. Paco whines to me, while Zeke puts his head

---

[13] Interestingly, it's mentioned in the leadership texts that it helps not to be too smart. Those with off-the-scale intelligence tend to make poor leaders. I suppose their constant weighing of options immobilizes them.
[14] (Kirkpatrick and Locke 1991)
[15] Bass 1990
[16] Pierce and Newstrom 2008

on Michaele's lap. Then Zeke will come to me to paw at me, and Paco will change stations over to Michaele and whine at her. They continue until one of us shows a chink in the armor, any sign of weakness. Maybe I'll pet Zeke's head and say, "All right, we'll go in a minute." He'll then go to Michaele to work on her.

The strategy is effective. Instead of spending another twenty minutes drinking our coffee and reading the news, we're out the door and on our way to the park with two furry bundles of energy. The strategy works because they persevere and gradually overcome our inertia. On some rainy days I swear if it weren't for the dogs we wouldn't leave the house at all.

Another metaphor about the power of persistence is the story of two neighbors digging wells. A piece of raw land was sold to two people, and each got half on which to build their homes. It was a rural area so they each needed to dig a well for water. The first man chose a spot and started digging. After about ten feet, he hit some large rocks, so he began thinking that maybe he was in the wrong spot, so he chose another spot and started digging. After about seven feet in this new spot he hit some roots and gave up again, thinking that there must be an easier spot that he could find. Again and again he tried, digging holes of varying depths all over his property, but none yielded any success. In the meantime, his neighbor had chosen one initial spot to dig, hit the same layer of rocks, and worked hard to remove them. He dug another ten feet, hit a few more rocks, and removed them as well. Another ten feet after that he hit water. His well was up and running, producing pure aquifer goodness, while his neighbor had spent twice the energy and still hadn't gotten anywhere closer to his goal.

# Lesson

Certain personal traits matter for effective leadership. Among the important ones are persistence, assertiveness, self-confidence, and initiative. Do your best to nurture these in yourself. The more you can develop these traits, the more likely you will be seen as a leader (and the more effective you will be once you are a leader). Next time you think that you've given it all you've got, remember Zeke. If a seventy-five-pound dog can outpull and outwill a two-hundred-pound person, then you've probably got better odds than you think if you just stay with it and plant your feet. Learning some ninja moves probably wouldn't hurt either.

# 5

## Rebranding a Pit bull

*Courage to be who you are long enough
to change perceptions*

Part of being a leader is having the courage to be who you are long enough to change people's perceptions. We all have different skills and different strengths to offer, but often there is an immense pressure to conform to some concept of "normal." The problem with caving to this pressure and trying to just *fit in* is that you don't *stand out*, by definition. If you spend all your time trying to conform to what you think is normal, then you will be actively working against being a leader, as you will just blend in with the crowd. You'll be just another "normal" person. There's nothing inherently wrong with this, of course, but we're after excellence and improvement, not merely status quo.

In the first weeks after Hurricane Katrina, Michaele and I evacuated with her family to the same friend's ranch outside of Houston where Paco had been found a short six months earlier. We had only been dating for a few weeks at this point, and here I was living under the same roof as her whole family. There were eleven of us in all who had caravanned from Louisiana to Texas— six people and five dogs. Michaele's mom, Kathy, is a dog lover from way back. When I had been shown the family photo albums she had spoken of Bam Bam, her childhood dachshund, just like any other member of the family. However, at this point she wasn't so sure about poor Zeke. He's officially a mutt—an inner-city pound dog. But he *looks* like a pit bull.[17] Somewhere back there he has some strong heritage. This in itself is not surprising as pit mixes make up the majority of pound dogs in the New Orleans area.

Kathy heard from Michaele that I had a pit bull and was concerned to be sharing a house with this beast (the fact that one of our first dates was on my motorcycle probably didn't help my reputation nor Zeke's). She hadn't really spent too much time with him—only a quick introduction—so she was a bit suspicious. Unfortunately, Staffordshire terriers and pit bulls have been unduly demonized in the press, and most people accept the stereotype without a second thought. I, too, was guilty of this before I adopted Zeke.

Kathy, like so many people, didn't know that the breed was actually considered a "nanny dog" in frontier times, as they protected the kids against wild animals.

Zeke had his work cut out for him. He was accused of being a threat before he walked in the door. Yet I wasn't worried. I knew Zeke to be a big goofy marshmallow of a dog who loves everybody, and I was interested to see how this would unfold.

We arrived late at night in Houston, the trip lasting a grueling eighteen hours instead of the typical six. The next morning Zeke went about his normal routine, making the rounds to get his back scratched. He stopped to put

---

[17] Every vet we've ever used—over six—has classified him as a mutt.

his bowling ball head in Kathy's lap and turned on the charm. He looked up at her with soft round eyes and wagged his tail. This earned him a smile and a polite pat on the head. By noon she was beginning to think that maybe he wasn't so scary after all. In the evening she was wondering why this breed had such a horrible reputation. And come bed time, she shocked us all by insisting that Zeke come and sleep on the bed with her.

Zeke won her over just by continuing to be himself. There was no need for him to be anything else to change her opinion and make her question her original bias against him. To this day he continues to display all of the positive qualities that this breed is known for (by those who take the time to actually get to know one): he's a big, roly-poly clown with a simple and bright outlook on life who loves everyone. Often we joke that we should have named him Ferdinand, after the bull in the children's book of the same name. Ferdinand was bred to be a fighting bull, but instead he preferred to sit under a shady tree sniffing flowers. Zeke *is* Ferdinand, choosing to sniff or quietly munch on the plants at the park rather than wrestle around with other dogs or live up to some ridiculous media image of a pit bull.

In San Francisco there is an organization called BADRAP, an acronym for Bay Area Dog Owners Responsible About Pit Bulls. It operates a rescue center for abused pit bulls where the dogs are rehabilitated and put into loving homes. Unfortunately, some animals have been abused so horribly that they can no longer safely be around people or other dogs. Their previous owners—the true monsters—broke their spirit and personality. But the best dogs, the ones whose true loving and clownish personalities stand out despite a history of abuse, are designated "ambassadors of the breed." They represent the true qualities of the breed to the public and counteract biased perceptions. Of course there are certainly animals of this breed that have been turned vicious by their owners, but as a breed they are consistently have some of the best temperaments. According to the American Temperament Test Society,[18] American Pit Bulls have an 86 percent pass rate on their standard

---

[18] http://www.atts.org/stats1.html

temperament test, which is higher than most dogs, including beagles, basset hounds, Chihuahuas, and golden retrievers!

Most recently, the media coverage of the fate of Michael Vick's dogs has helped change many people's opinions about this breed. They see that even in the worst of situations, most of these dogs can be brought back with love and care. They can be rehabilitated and showcase their true warm selves. Unfortunately, there is a set bias against the breed. On a recent trip to the Smithsonian's American History Museum, Michaele and I happened upon an exhibit detailing H. Nelson Jackson's completion of the first transcontinental automobile trip.[19] We were delighted to see that his companion (and marketing mascot) was a dog named Bud, clearly identifiable from original pictures and a plaster reproduction as a pit bull. However, the museum sign indicated he was a bull dog. Now there's a big difference between a bull dog and a pit bull.[20] It angered and saddened us to think that even the venerable Smithsonian seemed to have a bias against the breed. Was someone concerned about a public backlash if this faithful and famous dog was actually identified correctly as a pit bull? Would mothers cover their children's eyes with a protective hand, fearful their progeny might actually see a pit bull cast in a positive light?[21]

The point is that generally "public opinion" is wrong. So why spend so much time, energy, and worry, trying to conform to what public opinion thinks you should be doing with yourself and how you should be doing it?

Recently I saw a handwritten sign posted behind the counter at a coffee shop. It said, "In a world where you can be anything you want, why not be yourself?" This is a lesson that true leaders know well and live every day. They have the courage to be themselves and to believe in themselves. They spend less time worrying about how they might stack up against conventional

---

[19] http://americanhistory.si.edu/onthemove/exhibition/exhibition_7_2.html
[20] Go ahead and Google images of both. I'll wait.
[21] Of course, there's always the possibility that the museum just made an innocent mistake, but that seems unlikely.

views and more time doing what they feel is right. Eventually, when you are true to yourself and your interests, those who doubted you or were biased against you should come around. And those who don't would probably never have been satisfied anyway, so why worry about them?

Be real, be authentic, be enthusiastic about what you believe is right. Temper this with humility. Your drive, coupled with the reactions and responses of others, helps to shape who you are. Be grateful to others for their feedback because it makes you grow. But don't always assume they are right.

# Lesson

**Don't put too much stock in opinions of what others expect you to be. Have the courage to be yourself and work toward what you believe in. If Zeke could change Kathy's opinion of him from dangerous dog to snuggly bed buddy in twelve hours, chances are pretty good that you can change people's perceptions too.**

# 6

# The Stare

*The drive of a leader*

If you want to see focus—real focus—look into the eyes of a herding dog with a job to do. You will see a burning intensity that exists in few other places. Paco is bred to herd cattle, so he has "the stare." This stare is shared by most dogs who are supposed to tend animals. I see it in other blue heelers and sheep herding breeds at the park. When these dogs have a job to do, they have an intense focus. It's an expression of complete engagement with the task at hand. Until that task is complete, nothing else matters.

Paco has certain triggers for activating his stare. Every night at six he uses it to tell me it's dinner time. Or he may see me holding his leash, or hear the words "walk" or "beach." When the mood strikes me to tease him, I'll speak to him in similar-sounding words: "Paco, do you hear me as I *talk* to *each* of you?" It drives him crazy. The days of spelling out words are gone too. He knows what w-a-l-k means. Now we have to get creative to trick him, and we sound ridiculous in the process: "Michaele, would you want to sashay down to the ocean with the animals in a little while?"

When we leave for a walk, his initial frenzy to get out the door starts to become focused. As we get closer to the beach he becomes more single-minded. His little eyes dart to the ball thrower in my hand, then up to me expectantly. He pulls forward on the leash, legs shaking with anticipation. We cross over the final street to where the beach sand spills out onto the pavement. I tell him to sit, the leash comes off...and he becomes a ball-retrieving machine!

Once I pull out the tennis ball and show it to him, his eyes don't leave it. He'll hear me give him commands such as "sit" and "stay," but it's clear they are just an annoyance. The stare is so intense, his focus so pointed and laser-like, that when I move the ball even half an inch his muscles tense and his eyes widen, showing the whites. All that exists in his world right now is the ball. You could drop a steak next to him and he wouldn't notice.

If I could harness even half of this intensity and focus, I could have written this book in a week. In a world of increasing distractions and demands on our attention it is worth reminding ourselves what can be accomplished with a little bit of concentration. By turning off the phone for a few hours, getting away from the house for the afternoon, or closing the office door and putting on some classical music, we can realize significant results.

Looking back to the personality traits that scholars[22] have identified as central to effective leadership, many of them seem to define Paco to a T:

- **Drive:** *The ability to put forth a sustained high-level effort.* See tennis ball obsession in previous paragraph.

---

[22] Kirkpatrick and Locke 1991

- **Achievement**: *The ability to receive enjoyment and satisfaction from completing challenging tasks.* Did I mention we have to actually seek out cognitive games for dogs to keep Paco's overactive little brain occupied?

- **Ambition**: *The desire to get ahead.* We can't walk Paco without him pulling forward on the leash. He's hard-wired to be first at everything: first out the door, first on the walk, first back in the car, first back in the house.

- **Energy**: *Embodying the qualities of endless stamina, liveliness, and restlessness.* Paco can't even sleep restfully. Nine times out of ten when I happen to look at him in the middle of the night he's lying on his bed, staring back at me. I wonder if he even sleeps.

- **Tenacity**: *The ability to push through obstacles to achieve a goal.* Paco hasn't ever let a little thing like our laziness, exhaustion, or occupation with another task get in the way of him getting his dinner exactly at six o'clock. He'll whimper and pester us until we give in and feed him.

- **Initiative**: *Not simply waiting for an opportunity to arise, but actively going out and creating it.* See previous bullet point. He doesn't wait to be fed; he creates the opportunity to make it happen.

A friend told me that the best advice he ever received was to "focus on the end of the tunnel." In a time of personal difficulty, his mentor told him that there will always be people who try to throw him off of his path or distract him with side issues. These people are the "graffiti" on the sides of the tunnel. They pull your energy and attention away from the end of the tunnel—your true goal. If you spend all your time being distracted by the comments, complaints, gossiping, antics, and rumors of others then you will never get to where you want to go.

# Lesson

After you have defined your goals, focus on obtaining them. Do your best to ignore the commentary and criticisms of others and concentrate your energy into creating intensity to complete your task and obtain your goal. Keep in mind the qualities of drive, achievement orientation, ambition, energy, tenacity, and initiative. If you are unsure what any one of these looks like, watch a herding dog in action.

# 7

# OK, Now This

## *Open-mindedness*

As we go about our daily lives, we carry with us mental models. These models are based on what we have seen, heard, and experienced so far in our lives. They provide a framework through which we make sense of the world. As the information and technological revolution continues to dissolve borders, we are all exposed to more and more information which we must somehow integrate into our mental models (or simply discard and ignore—I think we all have seen this happen). Our existing mental models become outdated and no longer adequate to incorporate new, and often conflicting, information. Information evolves, situations shift, and in order to continue to function efficiently we need to continually question, update, and reconsider our mental models. They need to remain flexible. This is why we say, "Keep an open mind."

When people started looking at the personality traits of individuals commonly seen as leaders, a popular framework was developed to organize and make sense of those traits. Called the Big Five typology of personality,[23] it includes neuroticism, extraversion, agreeableness, conscientiousness, and openness to experience. Perhaps predictably, the only one of these five that was negatively correlated with leadership effectiveness was neuroticism. That is, the more neurotic an individual, the less likely he is to be an effective leader or be perceived as one by others (sorry, Paco).

But the other four were thought to be positively correlated with effective leadership. Generally, the more extroverted, open, agreeable, and conscientious one is, the more likely she will be an effective leader and be seen as such by others. Interestingly, the one factor with the highest positive correlation with leadership was openness to new experiences, which was associated with creativity and divergent thinking.[24]

This openness to experience is inherent in the life of a dog. I call it "Ok, now this." A common concept in Buddhism, the idea is to take life as it comes and live in the moment. As each moment arises—good or bad—it is accepted with an attitude of "ok, now this." Stuck at the DMV with number 356 when they are now serving number 212? *Ok, now I'm experiencing this.* Find a twenty-dollar bill on the sidewalk? *Ok, now this.* The idea is to observe experience without getting too wrapped up in it and without applying our past biases and preconceived notions to how we react. This flexibility and openness to new situations makes for a more effective leader. Part of this is keeping an open mind, of course, but there is more to it than that.

There are times when everything changes for us, and we are forced to confront and adapt to a new situation. Having a bit of a nomadic soul myself,

---

[23] Tupes and Christal 1961, Norman 1963
[24] Judge, et al. 2002

I've moved over a dozen times since college. Most of the decisions to relocate were voluntary, but some, like the one to California after Hurricane Katrina, were dropped suddenly in my lap. I've watched the dogs during our last five years of moves and noticed some key strategies they use to adapt to new circumstances.

Each time we move, the dogs embrace the new situation. They don't fight it. By adopting an attitude of "Ok, now this," they quickly move from what used to be to what is right now. By not clinging to what was, or comparing new to old, they do just fine. There is no let down or feeling sorry for what was and how the new doesn't measure up. The dogs go through four distinct phases of adjusting: confronting, understanding, accepting, and adapting strategy.

It has occurred to me that each time we load them up in the car and hop on the highway they don't know if they are going for a quick trip or moving across country. With this constant uncertainty, they openly confront whatever is outside the door when I let them out. They burst forth, ready to see where they are and what it has to offer them (hopefully unwitting squirrels or cats). Judging by their enthusiasm you'd think they expected a land of beef jerky trees and liver treat lawns.

A few months after our move, my wife's parents came to visit us in Belgium. The dogs, of course, were thrilled to see them (My mother-in-law is affectionately known to the dogs as "the cookie lady" for her constant supply of treats). After Kathy and Jon left, the dogs still expected to see them everywhere. When you think about it from their perspective, why not? They didn't know that her parents had flown back home. Every person walking down the street or coming through a door *might* be them. The dogs had a constant air of being ready and open to whatever situation might come their way.

The second phase they go through is understanding. From the moment we open a door to a new apartment, the dogs rush in, make a tour of the place, and try to get a feel for it. They explore and attempt to understand everything they can about it: *Ok, here's the door to the back. Here's the comfortable napping rug. There's the water bowl.* They take in as much as they can about their new situation. By looking for the key elements that they need to survive, they don't fret too much about where they are located. Maybe the water bowl is in the pantry in one place. In the next apartment it's in the kitchen, and in a third they find it in the guest bathroom. As long as there *is* a water bowl, they're happy.

After understanding, they move on to accepting. This may take a few days, but before long they settle in and realize that this is the new normal. They take what they know and adjust their strategies to get what they want. If there's a door that opens directly to the outside, that's where Paco goes to sit and yip to be let out. If we're on the fourteenth floor and the only door out is to the hallway, he knows that is where he needs to sit to tell us. Zeke will locate the new hiding place for the basket of toys and realize that when he wants to rummage around for something to play with, that's where he has to go now.

In no time I watched the dogs find the similarities to the old situation— for instance, a daily walk to a grassy area, morning and evening feeding times, and the placement of their beds in the corners of the bedroom. Once recognized, they take comfort in those similarities, making the best of what was completely new and unfamiliar.

According to leadership research, a common cause of executive derailment is the inability to adapt. Derailment refers to situations when a person is performing well and showing all signs of moving up the ladder and then all of a sudden gets thrown off, stagnating or tanking their career. Their little engine that could suddenly can't and "derails" from the fast track. Failure to adapt to new cultures, situations, and surroundings are common reasons. Whether it is the technology or the direction of the company, the bus has left and they aren't on it. Leadership effectiveness isn't solely based on the leader as an individual. It's also dependent on environmental factors and the receptiveness of the followers. When everything around a leader changes and she stays the same, her ability to lead will be severely tested.

A vivid example of this is what happened to Hosni Mubarak in Egypt during the eighteen-day protests that ended on February 11, 2011. The Egyptian people, motivated by the successful protests in Tunisia, gathered en masse and pressed for Mubarak to step down. As the weeks of protest progressed, the situation was clear: Mubarak had to go. It seemed the only one who didn't know this was Mubarak himself. Countries all over the globe—even allies such as the US—were calling for him to acquiesce to the demands of the people. His followers had changed. The situation had changed. His leadership had *not* changed, and that was the problem. He was unable to adapt to the new environment and demands of his followers and he lost his position.

If you have trouble adapting to change, chances are you try unsuccessfully to apply old solutions to new problems. You press on doing what you've always done, hoping that will solve the problem. The thinking goes, *I'll do what I've always done, but I'll just try harder and do more of it! That'll work!*

In business school we studied the ultimate example of this. When coal-powered ships began to replace wind-powered vessels, one old-time nautical builder responded to the threat by simply putting more and more sails on his boats. He reasoned that if some sails were good, more were better. The result was a ridiculous looking and inefficient vessel that was almost impossible to operate. This was clearly no threat to the new coal-powered ship builders, and the company soon faded into obscurity.

# Lesson

New situations and new challenges can be met and adapted to slowly and gradually. If you are not very adaptable, try looking for similar elements in the new situation that you might be familiar with. Use the dogs' strategy of confronting the changes head on, understanding what they are and what they mean to you, accepting them, and adapting to the new demands. Even if you are not very good at this technique at first, you will be better than you were, and this will improve your chances for success in the new situation. When the situation demands it, change your strategy to remain competitive.

# 8

Catching the Fast Dog
at the Park

*Compete where you naturally excel*

For an effective strategy you must know your strengths and use them to your advantage. Just because we see others excel using a certain approach does not mean that it will work for us. Our situation might be different and not suitable for their strategy. Or we may have a different set of skills that don't allow us to tackle the problem in the same way they did. Their strategy might capitalize on their strengths—ones which we don't have. In order to succeed, we must choose the right approach for us. To do that requires a good understanding of our own strengths and weaknesses.

Paco chooses his strategy based on what he knows to be his strongest traits. He's quick and agile and uses this as his main competitive edge over other dogs. Whether his objective is a treat, outrunning another dog at the park, or motivating us to take him for a walk, he uses his speed to get what he wants. Zeke, on the other hand, is built like a powerful little freight train. He chooses strategies where his bulk and mass can be of utmost advantage.

Periodically we come across a dog that just loves to be chased. "Oh yeah," its owner will say, "he's a runner." It doesn't take much to goad our dogs into pursuing the this runner at top speed in loops around the park. In most cases the lead dog will streak in a wide circle, staying to the confines of the park. When they were young and new to the game, both Zeke and Paco stayed right behind in hot pursuit. It didn't take long for Zeke to realize that he never has a chance with this direct approach. As he became more experienced, his strategy changed. Now he veers off toward the center of the curve formed by the lead dog, triangulating to cut him off. Heading to where he anticipates the runner will be, Zeke appears out of nowhere to T-bone the other dog and send it rolling across the grass with a yelp. Those who witness the brutal collision usually cringe and offer up an, "Oh, *man!*" Zeke wins by capitalizing on his strength and power.

Paco, on the other hand, couldn't knock over a folding chair. Instead, he uses his speed to stay at the heels of the lead dog and chase him directly. Sometimes he reaches the dog before Zeke's triangulation tackle is complete, and other times he arrives on the scene after the game is over. I've never seen Paco attempt Zeke's strategy, and Zeke gave up trying to compete through direct chase a long time ago. These days he won't even chase a tennis ball unless I specifically tell Paco to sit and that "It's Zeke's turn." He knows he can't outrun Paco, so why try? Each one uses a strategy that capitalizes on what they do best to maximize the chance of winning.

# Lesson

Observe yourself, and start to recognize your own strengths. Ask others to comment on what they see as your strengths, as sometimes they are hard to see for yourself. Another great resource is the StrengthsFinder designed by Gallup, which provides a thorough report of your strengths after a brief test. When you are competing, consider how you might use your strengths to your advantage. A keen awareness of your core competencies and strengths will help you come up with more successful strategies.

# 9

# Zeke, Inc.

*Create and nurture a personal brand*

Once you get comfortable with your strengths, the next step is to come up with your own personal brand. Although it isn't always fun to think of marketing yourself, promoting a certain authentic image is a solid way to advance yourself. A personal brand is simply the "You" that you present to the outside world. It is a consistent way that you are known to others. These days, this concept is more popular—and important—than ever. Social media dominates, and your public profile presents you to the outside world. If you don't take active control of it, you run the risk of an image that is scattered—or worse. Before the days of Internet ubiquity, your personal brand came through at work and in other face-to-face interactions that were easier to manage.

Many opportunities exist to develop how you are seen by others. But there are ways to lose control as well. One is by presenting an incoherent or contradictory personal brand online. If you have a Facebook account, web page, blog, or even just e-mail you are already developing a personal brand whether you know it or not. If you consciously and deliberately develop it, your brand will help distinguish you from the crowd. Others will be more likely to remember you as unique.

Think about who will be viewing your "brand" online and what impression you'd like them to come away with. Are you trying to appear professional? Creative and spontaneous? Traditional and reliable? A family person? A party person? The stakes are clearly higher these days as it isn't as easy to have a different brand for each audience. A friend of mine has a Facebook account connected not only to his family and friends but to his boss and his boss's children. Gone are the days where you can put the kids "to bed" and assume a party personality for the night. Now someone may post pictures of that night where your grandmother, your kids, and your boss might see them. To make matters worse, what ends up online lives forever. New technology has made it harder and harder to leave the past behind and create a new persona.

What matters here is coherence. Whatever brand you decide to display, take some time to ensure that there is a consistent flow through all of the channels you use to present it. If you present a party-girl personality on Facebook, a dedicated mom approach on Flickr, and a ruthless executive persona on LinkedIn, you may send some mixed messages.

Believe it or not, even my dogs are starting to see the power behind developing a personal brand. They're naturals at it. Zeke's got it down more than Paco, who is still trying to figure out what works best. For instance Zeke has mastered the "big, goofy, droopy dope who loves everyone" brand. He charms us and our guests by plodding over and sitting on the lap of anyone who's on the floor (no small event at eighty pounds—he's not exactly a lap dog). His signature move to get your attention is plopping his chin on your leg, a chair, or the couch, while he gawks up at you as if he just can't hold his big bowling ball head up any longer. Then, while staring at you with the biggest eyes he can make, he drops his floppy ears and makes *the noise*. It comes from so far back in his throat that it isn't so much a voice as a vibration: *Mrrrrr...Mrrrrrr...*

Once this ridiculous display wins you over, and you reach for him, he quickly pulls away. It's so fast it's startling. *How can this comatose and vibrating lump of dog react so quickly?* As soon as you draw your hand back, his head returns to its original location, ears and eyes droop, and the game starts up all over again: *Mrrrrrr...Mrrrrrr...*He doesn't want to be patted. He wants you up—to feed him, let him out, or play with him. It seems endless until you give in. He is frequently successful because his methods completely fit with his personal brand: slow, deliberate, stubborn, heavy, and dopey. *It's just Zeke being Zeke again.*

Paco watches Zeke get what he wants using this approach and decides to try it himself. At dinner time he walks up, rests his small pointy head lightly on the corner of the couch, and stares at us with his caffeinated little eyes. He looks like a coiled spring ready to burst. It's hilarious. He has none of Zeke's heavy presence. In its place is a light and wiry frame with huge ears sticking straight up in the air, tail high, wagging briskly. Michaele and I can't keep a straight face. We even point derisively at him. "That's not you!" we say between bursts of laughter. "What are you trying to do?"

Paco's antics don't work because it doesn't fit with his personal brand. He's naturally high-strung, shrill, and light on his feet. As a herding dog whose neuroses overflow (no doubt due in part to a premature separation from his mother) using Zeke's "look at how pathetic and droopy and sad I am" approach is a complete failure for him. We dismiss it as an obvious attempt at imitation, and he doesn't get what he's after. Although impressive in its imitation, his strategy didn't fit with his otherwise strong personal brand.

# Lesson

Whether or not you are aware of it, some form of a personal brand is being presented to the outside world: to your family, friends, coworkers, and the online community. Using what you have learned about your strengths, start to think about what kind of brand you want to present, and then look to see if that is indeed what you are presenting. Ask others how you appear on your blog, website, and profile, and start to deliberately craft your personal brand across all channels. Use that style to distinguish yourself from others. Be careful of presenting mixed messages or using someone else's brand and technique too blatantly, as obvious imitation doesn't get you where you want to be.

# 10

# Shoe Leather
*Developing personal resilience*

One of my favorite stories about personal resiliency is adopted from an Indian sage named Ramana Maharshi. A man is troubled with his difficult life and sets out to find the wisest monk for advice on how to deal with his problems. He eventually finds the wise old sage, who asks him what's wrong.

> "Every day I encounter hardship in my family life, in my work life, everywhere!" the man exclaims. "Why are other people so difficult, and why is it that everything seems to be working against me getting what I want?"

> "I see," the monk replies calmly. "Let me ask you—how far did you travel to see me today?"

Confused, the man thinks and responds, "I walked for about five hours."

"Was the road here smooth?"

"What do you mean?" the man asked.

"Did you encounter rocks and sticks on the road?"

"Yes, of course I did—you live in the middle of the woods connected by nothing but a footpath for miles."

"And how do your feet feel?" the monk asked with an expression of concern.

"Fine, I guess."

"The rocks and sticks and rough path—they didn't injure the soles of your feet?"

"No."

"Why not?"

The man thought for a minute. "Well, to begin with, I'm wearing shoes, of course."

"I see," replied the monk, slowly nodding his head. "And why didn't you just go barefoot?"

"Because I knew the road was rough."

"But why not cover the path from here to there in leather? Better yet, why not cover the whole world in leather? Then you wouldn't have to wear any shoes and you'd feel more free."

The man began to think if maybe he found the wrong monk. "Well, that's just a crazy idea. It's silly—trying to cover the whole world in leather! Not only is it crazy—it's impossible!"

"Exactly," replied the monk, and he slowly turned and walked away.

Do you see? When we look to change others and the situation around us, we are attempting to cover the world with leather. Instead of growing a thick skin and becoming resilient (putting on shoes), we try to control that which is outside of us simply because we have discomfort. Not only is it futile to try to do this, it's selfish. Why should everything else change for our whims?

While you may have limited success altering a few outside factors, it takes a lot of effort and energy and will never really pay off in the long run. The better way to prepare yourself and to deal with the external difficulties, the "sticks and stones" on the road of life, is to outfit yourself with a good pair of shoes that you can then take with you everywhere you go.

This pair of shoes is personal resilience. Once you develop and cultivate a healthy attitude and some perspective and endurance, you are better prepared to deal with troubles as they arise. Like a Boy Scout, you are always prepared. And you can take this ability with you everywhere. Work on yourself rather than trying to change the rest of the world to achieve the best results with the least effort. As hard as it is to look inside and change your habits, it's easier than trying to change everyone else's.

For animals who crave routine, my dogs are very resilient. They have learned to adapt to new places, new routines, and new people as we have moved them all over the world. At first they clearly had difficulties. Zeke tore apart pillows when he was left alone, and Paco peed with nervousness when he met strangers. Over time they learned to adapt themselves and deal with difficulties as they arose. With each move it happened more quickly. The new routine—new parks to walk to, new distances from the door of the house or apartment to the outside area where it was OK to go to the bathroom—was fine by them. Instead of trying to change their situation and avoid the difficulties, they developed thick skin and just rolled with the changes.

Resilience is a key quality of leadership, as most worthwhile initiatives require time, patience, and tenacity. Tenacity has been identified as one of the personal traits of effective leaders.[25] For example, several clients of mine have implemented new software systems in order to become more productive. Typically this involves a long process of determining the shortcomings of the existing system, the requirements of its replacement, and the attributes of each alternate system on the market. Then the real fun starts as all users have to be trained on how to use it and why it's worthwhile. It can take several months to over a year to make the full transition from one system to another. Those clients who do not have tenacity and resilience often became frustrated early on in the process. Some give up. Others only put minimal effort into each stage, resulting in a much less effective end product. One client didn't have the energy to define what their needs really were and as a result ended up with an expensive system they didn't need. To add insult to injury, the staff soon realized that the new software was wrong and simply refused to learn it. The result, of course, was that the whole endeavor was a waste of time, money, and effort.

Tenacious leaders keep pushing through. They adapt to difficulties they encountered as they went along. Their ability to bounce back from setbacks and keep a positive forward momentum leads to long-term positive benefits as the right system is chosen, the employees effectively trained, and the improvements realized.

In a review of ten studies in effective leader qualities, the quality of resilience comes up again and again in different forms. It appears in self-confidence, which was identified in 80 percent of the studies as one of the most important qualities. It also is part of the traits of persistence, determination, adaptability, adjustment, tenacity, and stress tolerance, each found to be components of effective leader personalities. The evidence is compelling: the more you can work on your personal resilience, the better a leader you will be.

---

[25] Kirkpatrick and Locke 1991

# Lesson

Rather than trying to change the rest of the world to suit your preferences, learn to develop personal resiliency and tenacity so that you can better deal with inevitable difficulties and setbacks. The effort you put in to become more resilient will pay off many times through more effective and desirable results. Take Ramana Maharshi's advice: "Wanting to reform the world without discovering one's true self is like trying to cover the world with leather to avoid the pain of walking on stones and thorns. It is much simpler to wear shoes."[26]

---

[26] "teaspout" 2008

# 11

$\Longleftrightarrow$

# Get the Cookie, Paco!

*Turning neuroticism into determination*

My dogs are very different from each other. As a herding dog, Paco has lots of energy and is very vocal. Zeke is more of a slow-moving, sausage-shaped clown. Although they stand shoulder-to-shoulder the same height, Zeke is solid and weighs almost twice as much as Paco. Their differences are never clearer than when I give them a rawhide bone to chew on and pass the time. "Want a cookie?" I'll say, and both dogs will jump up even from the deepest slumber and race to my side.

After gently taking it from my hand, Zeke will immediately find a comfortable place on the rug,[27] plop down, and just start chewing the bone. His

---

[27] In the sun, if possible. If there's sunlight hitting the floor, he'll find it.

powerful jaws make short work of it. In fact, when he's chewing on a hard rubber toy, the muscles from his jaws will reach all the way to the crown of his head and flex so hard that they push his eyeballs out a little. It looks painful and certainly disturbing at first until you realize how content he is. With the rest of the world faded off into a haze, he's in the zone. The only thing important to him now is chewing that whole bone up.

Paco, on the other hand, is more of a showman. He needs an audience and recognition. The cookie is a prop in a performance to get our attention. No sooner is it snatched out of my hand before he spits it out like it was a mouse that just bit him on the tongue. He stares at it in disbelief, then up at me, head tilted and eyes wide. *Did you see that? This cookie fights back!* He approaches it with back legs stiff and front legs down in a playful pose. Will it nip him again? Nosing it gently, he springs back and yips at me. *Yes, I know, Paco, you have a cookie. Now just eat it.* If I ignore him at this point he'll lose interest in it, abandon it, and wander away. But if I play along and tell him, "Get the cookie, Paco! Get the cookie!" then he's thrilled and grabs the slightly moist rawhide to prance around some more. He'll try to get me to throw it in the other room, and if I don't oblige, he'll toss it there himself and look at back at me. *Look at what I have! Don't you want in on this? Aren't I amazing for having this?* Eventually, after much playing, attention, and praise, he'll usually settle down to slowly nibble. But boy, I have to earn my peace and quiet.

For Paco the cookie is a way to elicit praise and participation from us. In itself it isn't interesting, but it can be used to get attention. If he can't goad one of us into participating in his game, then it simply isn't worth the effort. There's no intrinsic motivation for him in eating it. He'll abandon it completely. For Zeke, on the other hand, the cookie itself is what is important. Not only does he ignore us from the moment he gets it, he effectively shuts out the outside world until he gulps the last slimy piece of it down his gullet. The cookie is its own reward; it is intrinsically motivating. Even if I interrupt Zeke from munching his cookie, he will (after shooting me a dirty look) calmly walk into another room where he will be undisturbed to get back to the task at hand.

Over the years of working as a management consultant I've noticed lots of clients and their employees who fall into either the Zeke or Paco approach to completing a task. Those in the Paco camp are recognition-oriented and use their task to draw attention. They may even leave the project or task aside completely if they think that they aren't getting enough praise, notice, or direction from others. One employee (let's call him Carl) I worked with had the task of devising a new inventory system for the warehouse. In the beginning, when the president of the company was giving him this assignment, Carl was very enthusiastic as he felt important enough to be chosen to complete this task. He loved the attention and promised to deliver in the required timeframe. In the next weeks, he made it known to all the other employees how he was asked by the boss and the outside consultant to create a more efficient warehouse inventory system.

However, after the initial wave of interest and focus on him had subsided he lost interest in the task. When asked about it a month later, he hadn't shown any progress. He was then told directly to get on it ("Get the cookie, Carl") and showed a brief burst of focus before abandoning it again. Eventually it had to be reassigned, and Carl had dropped a few pegs down in the eyes of his boss.

Then there are the people in the Zeke camp. These people are achievement-oriented. They jump on a task or idea, know exactly what needs to be done, and just settle in to do it. They produce results. We've all known a few, the ones who rise quickly in their jobs and seem to be more content with themselves. Not every task is enjoyable in itself, but these people always seem to get some measure of satisfaction from a good day's hard work. Completing the task is its own reward. Like Zeke, if they are distracted or thrown off the task, they quickly regroup and get back down to it again. They either rise within a company as star employees or go and strike out on their own. Some even become serial entrepreneurs, moving from one idea to another.

Again we turn to the scholarly literature on what traits make for effective leaders. In this case, we can see how Zeke's approach to the treat is a perfect example of three characteristics that have been found to be associated with effective leadership: achievement motivation, determination, and internal locus of control. When someone has achievement motivation it means that they have a strong drive to compete and succeed in life. It makes sense that having this trait, along with being very determined, would make one an effective leader. The last one, internal locus of control, refers to people who tend to believe that they are generally responsible for what happens to them in life. They don't blame circumstances outside of their control, but rather believe that they can make an effort and change their situation. An effective leader would tend to think that he can change things for the better, and then act on that belief.

Paco's behavior can best be described as neurotic, exhibited by his poor emotional adjustment, anxiety, insecurity, and need for affiliation (insistence we join him). This neuroticism has been found to be negatively correlated to leader emergence and effectiveness. In other words, the more neurotic you are, the less likely you will become a leader at all or be seen by others as an effective one.[28]

A leader, whether born or trained, tends to be more like Zeke. She will quickly realize that spending time worrying about the task, contemplating it too long, or trying to use it to get attention and praise is at best a distraction that delays the eventual completion of the task. What matters to her is achieving that goal through determined effort. At worst a neurotic approach can hold her back personally and professionally as she "stalls out" when others conclude she's either not capable of being a leader or simply not up to the challenge.

---

[28] Judge, et al. 2002

# Lesson

When you are faced with a task or have an idea of something that you'd like to do, put all of your energy and focus into completing it. Be aware when you are becoming sidetracked and using it solely to get attention or praise. The more neurotic your approach, and the more you use the task for ulterior motives such as politics or power games, the more likely you are to be perceived as a poor leader (or even a poor follower). If there's a challenge in front of you, realize that you have the power to make it happen. Mobilize resources if you need them. Buckle down and motivate yourself to achieve the goal. Just go get that cookie.

# 12

~~~

# One Mood, All the Time
*Emotional intelligence and self-awareness*

Aside from the occasional outburst over a bone or walk-induced hysteria, my dogs aren't very moody. They are very steady emotionally. In comparison, I feel like a wreck. I don't consider myself any moodier than the average person, but when I'm constantly around these even-keeled animals it's hard not to notice my moods.

Paco has an internal alarm clock set for around 7:30 a.m. If I'm still in bed he'll tiptoe up and stick his damp sponge of a nose in my face. My response depends on how I'm feeling. If I'm rested and refreshed, I reach out and pat his head to greet him with a "Hey there, Paco-Mole."[29] When I've had fitful slumber and need to sleep in, I push him away and lunge over angrily toward the center of the bed, grumbling about how "the dumb dog woke me up." Before I'm even fully awake, I know my mood.

The same is true when I take Zeke for a walk. When I'm in a positive state of mind and he's pulling on the leash, I gently correct him or allow him to pull me a little. But his little tugs drive me crazy when I'm already in a sour mood. Sharply pulling him back, I bark out his name *"Zeke!"* I immediately feel remorse. *I must be in a bad mood. Why?*

Having the ability to gauge your own moods is one of the components of emotional intelligence (EI). Emotional intelligence is a relatively recent construct and was suggested as an alternative (or complimentary) measurement to the traditional IQ or intelligence quotient. Although there are at least three different models for EI,[30] each centers around perceiving and managing emotions. Only in the last few decades have leadership researchers begun to study the role of emotions. What they've found is that emotions play a central role in the effectiveness of both individuals and organizations.

The term emotional intelligence was coined by two psychologists named Salovey and Mayer. They were studying why some smart people fail to succeed and found that many lacked the ability to accurately read their own emotions and those of others. They may have been bright, but they were insensitive and had poor interpersonal skills, which contributed detrimentally to their long-term success. The psychologists concluded that emotional intelligence is a set of skills that allow a person to accurately perceive emo-

---

[29] There is a history of silly nicknames for animals in my family. Usually these names evolve, or should I say devolve, from the pet's actual name. Shortly after I met Paco I started calling him Wacko because he was a manic little fur ball. Since he would pop back up every time you thought you had gotten rid of him, he reminded me of the classic Whack-a-Mole game, so I called him Wacko Mole. Next I dropped the Wacko part and simply called him Mole, because he reminded me of a rodent with his beady eyes and pointy whiskered nose. Paco-Mole is just a variant.
[30] Hughes, Ginnett and Curphy 2009

tions in themselves and others. Their model had four components: perceiving emotions, managing emotions, using emotions, and understanding emotions.

The more skilled she is in each of these components, the higher a leader's chance for success. If she can read her emotions and the emotions of others and can deduce their origins, she can better understand and manage a situation. As the building blocks of much human behavior, emotions hold the key to better leadership.

A key component of emotional intelligence is self-monitoring. Technically self-monitoring "refers to the individual's ability and motivation to manage how he or she presents her or himself to others as a function of the reading of the social cues emitted by others."[31] The better you can observe, and therefore monitor, your mood, the better you can begin to regulate that mood and align it with the current needs of the situation (and your followers) to produce the best results.

It can be difficult to objectively observe your own moods. Most of the time we are so wrapped up in the moment that our emotions are obscured. When things don't go our way, we blame factors beyond our control.[32] There's a common story about a boss who yells at his employee. That employee then goes home and shouts at his kids, who turn around and kick the dog. Unfortunately, a pet may be at the receiving end of frustrations that began somewhere else entirely.

Having a dog around is a great reminder to observe your own moods and to consider their origins. A pet's steady and reliable behavior can point out your own crazy emotional swings. As you start to understand your own

---

[31] Pierce and Newstrom 2008

[32] There are two interesting social psychology theories that apply here. The actor-observer bias states that when things don't go our way, we tend to blame situational factors ("I bet I didn't get a pay increase because my boss doesn't like me") but when we succeed, we tend to attribute that accomplishment solely to our own personal effort ("I earned that raise all by myself"). The fundamental attribution error states that when we observe the behavior of other people, we tend to attribute it to their own efforts ("He got into an accident because he's a bad driver") while we attribute situational factors to our own similar behavior ("I crashed my car because that guy cut me off!").

emotions, it becomes easier to perceive those of others. Once you can do this, you have a more complete assessment of your situation and can better navigate it. This leads to more positive outcomes not only for yourself, but for everyone. By aligning emotions and motivation, the results should also come with less effort, as you do not need to use brute force to push through your agenda.

# Lesson

Start to observe your moods. Pay attention to how you respond to your pet, family members, or coworkers on a daily basis. As you become better able to identify your moods, explore where they may have come from. The key is to be able to notice them from an outside perspective, to cultivate an internal voice that notices, "Huh, I guess I'm angry," instead of just being angry. The more you are able to understand yourself, the more you will understand others, and the easier relations will become, both at home and at work.

# 13

~~~

# "Zeke, Quit Licking Your Foot!"

*Changing tactics as the situation changes*

This should be an easy one. We've all been in the situation where no matter how hard we try, we can't seem to make progress on a certain task. For me it was when I took Real Number Analysis in college. I was a math major for a brief time and happy about it until I started seeing upside down A's and all kinds of other mysterious symbols in the class work. I stuck at it for a while, failing quizzes and falling behind. Finally I accepted reality, dropped the class, and switched my major to economics. While it can take us a while to see the light, it's usually obvious to those around us when we are fighting a losing battle. There's perseverance, and then there's making things worse. If I had stuck in that class I'm certain I would have failed and had to switch majors anyhow. So why stay?

As a management consultant I enjoyed my work, but I didn't see eye to eye with my superiors all the time. After working with a client for a few weeks, I would have ideas about how best to meet their needs, and often these suggestions would not mesh with the more universal approach of the company. As I liked and respected my coworkers, I tried to gently make my case over my years there. After some time I realized that I was not getting anywhere, and I left to find other employment. I could have stayed and kept hitting my head against that upper management wall, trying to wear them down. But I probably would have made my situation worse and only ended up bothering everyone. It wouldn't have done anyone any good.

The dogs, unfortunately, don't have quite as much perspective. Zeke, who most of the time is easygoing and laid back, turned his stubbornness into a self-damaging obsession shortly after our arrival in Brussels. Michaele and I had just signed a yearlong lease for an apartment in a small neighborhood away from the city center. We were lugging a dozen or so enormous suitcases from our current center-city apartment, making multiple trips back and forth as we didn't yet have a car. Every trip required several steps: down the tiny winding stairs of the old third floor apartment, out the door and over treacherous ancient cobblestones for several blocks, around tourists and into the underground subway station, which stank like a dirty litter box. Once we jammed on the train wielding our 150 pounds of bags, we jockeyed for a position with surprisingly spry retirees, and held on through the four stops to disembark. Then we pushed our way off with our cargo, dogs pulling left and right, and hauled our load up to street level before walking ten blocks uphill to the new apartment. It was draining.

On one of these trips we had to take the dogs too. We came off the train and got ready to trudge up out of the underground station. Michaele, always with a mind toward taking the healthy route, chose the stairs, with Paco bounding up next to her on the leash. Exhausted and lazy at this point, I lumbered on to the escalator so I could stand still for a moment. I had Zeke on the other end of the leash. He was hesitant for a moment but then jumped on the escalator, legs splayed wide for balance. When we reached the stop I noticed he made an awkward leap onto the pavement but thought nothing of it, and we started our inclined trek to the new place.

Fifteen minutes later the dogs entered the apartment for the first time and did their usual crazy run around for unfamiliar locations. As they explored every corner and spot on the floor, we dropped our bags and hobbled off to get some water in the kitchen. Michaele gave me a kiss goodbye and took off to make a run to IKEA to pick up some last-minute items while I started to unpack. Then I noticed something strange. There were little brown spots all over the pine wood floor. They were everywhere. I got down closer and noticed that they weren't so much brown as dark red. Blood. Little bits all over the floor. Immediately I checked out the dogs and found that Zeke had cracked a nail on his back foot like a walnut shell— right down the middle.

Thinking back to diagnose how this happened, I realized I had inadvertently caused it by taking him up the escalator. Poor Zeke. His nail probably split open right as we got to the street, which explains his huge leap off the moving stairs. But he never made a sound or showed any concern, not at the time and not up until that point. We both noticed his damaged foot at the same time, and from then on it got all of his attention.

For the next months he obsessed over it. Every day we'd disinfect it with a spray, wrap it, and protect it. When he wasn't walking, eating, or sleeping, he licked it obsessively. At the beginning we understood and let him nurse his wound. After a few weeks passed and he didn't let up, we would say gently, "Zeke...leave it." When it still didn't stop a month later we stepped up the tone. We'd hear this wet and tonguey sound from the other room, like someone stirring a big tub of yogurt slowly with a wooden spoon: *Sschlloop... sschlloop...sschlloop...sschlloop.* It was almost like the sound a grandfather clock would make ticking off the seconds if it were made entirely of moist tongue, the pendulum *sschllooping* back and forth as it stuck moistly to the sides of its fleshy, humid case. "*Zeke!*" we'd snap. "Leave your foot alone!"

The wound healed...slowly. I'm convinced it took three times as long because he kept bothering it every chance he got. He would actively work against his immune system by tearing off scabs and keeping the whole moist and bacteria-laden. We even tried to deter him by putting an old dingy white athletic sock over his foot, gently taping the top up so it wouldn't slide off. Well, it didn't stop Zeke—he just *sschlooped* through the sock, gradually marinating it in saliva. He finally stopped a few months after it was totally healed.

Zeke took the appropriate response to a situation—licking his wounds—and persisted until it was harmful. Eventually it became destructive. He didn't recognize that the response no longer fit the situation. There are many examples when we do this same type of thing. Consider the student in class who feels uncomfortable and cracks a joke, getting a laugh as a response from the rest of the class. This works well to break the ice, particularly the first time the class meets, but eventually, if he keeps it up, it becomes irritating to those around him and can end up isolating him socially.

The mother who dotes on her child is to be commended, but there is a time to let go and loosen the grip. Many recent articles discuss "helicopter parents" who hover around their kids even through college and wait on them hand and foot, even fighting their battles for them. This support and protection is valuable when a child is small but if continued may actually be crippling to the young adult. The classic enabler is one who allows others to continue destructive behavior through what looks like support. In the beginning, that support was probably the right thing to do, but in the wrong circumstances it may continue the behavior that it was trying to prevent.

In a study concerning the negative side of leader-follower relationships, researchers found that one of the five factors that contributes to bad leader-follower relations is the "unwillingness to let go" on the part of the leader.[33] In this case, the leader knows that he is no longer effective but simply holds on to his position (and power) long past the point where he should have let go. The study proposes a few psychological reasons for why this might be. The leader's ego may get in the way as he identifies too much with his position: *If I'm not VP of Sales for the Western Europe region, then what am I?* Or he may fear reprisals from those he wronged while he was in power. This is the idea that the stones you throw on the way up always find you on the way down. Finally, he may simply fear the loss of his legacy and associate his loss of position with a slow slide into obscurity.

In any case, whether you look at it from a psychological or physical perspective, holding on too long can produce pain and negative consequences.

---

[33] Clements and Washbush 1999

# Lesson

Know when to move on and when the response to a situation no longer fits it. Zeke's wound-licking was helpful at first. But at a certain point it just prolonged the wound and kept it from healing. Studies indicate that the inability of a leader to let go when he should leads to negative consequences not only for that leader, but for the followers and the organization as a whole. Try to keep an objective eye on your response to a situation if you think what worked before is no longer working. Solicit advice from a trusted advisor, and try to make the best decision not only for yourself, but for others as well.

# II

# Working with Others

In this second section the focus is how to interact and work with others effectively, as leadership "is an influence relationship among leaders and followers who intend real changes and outcomes that reflect their shared purposes.[34]"

It's easy to think of leadership as a static concept. *The leadership they provided was adequate.* Research on the subject has evolved and suggests that it is more of a dynamic, fluid process. It is, as defined above, an influence relationship, one that can be handled deftly or clumsily. For this reason, learning how to best interact with others is central to becoming an effective leader.

---

[34] Daft 2005

We'll look at what dog park interactions can teach us about dealing with new people, how high school math can help you lead a team, and why it helps to have friends with money. We'll also consider how dog adoption is similar to manager-employee relationships, how dogs use their own form of social networking, and the power of followership.

# 14

&—3

# Forget Beer—Dogs Are the Real Social Lubricant

*Directing and aligning the efforts of others*

Managers and leaders are often confused with each other. The two are not synonymous, and each has a unique function in the organization:

> Managers are thinkers and workers and doers. Leadership is concerned instead with communicating the vision and developing a shared culture and set of core values that can lead to the desired future state...whereas the vision describes the destination, the culture and values help

define the journey toward it. Leadership focuses on getting everyone lined up in the same direction.[35]

Leaders bring people together. They motivate others to work in the same direction and accomplish common goals. "A leader…sets the basis for relationships within the group, and thereby can affect outcomes."[36] A leader's "failure to provide goal orientations [common direction toward a goal] within the group led to antagonism, tension, and absenteeism."[37] When everyone is unclear on the common goal and how to exert effort to achieve it, inefficiencies emerge and in the worst case, things fall apart. The challenge is to provide the vision and to motivate others to work toward the same ends.

Dogs are masters at bringing people together and lowering inhibitions. They are a "social lubricant" without the hangover of alcohol. Anyone who has ever been to a dog park has seen this in action. At Coliseum Square, the dog park in New Orleans where I met my wife, people gather every day after work to let their dogs play. One of the fastest ways to meet someone is when you are jointly embarrassed by your dogs' behavior. You dog owners out there know exactly what I'm talking about. Even good behavior can be grounds for an ice-breaking conversation. It worked for me and Michaele. Back when we were only friendly strangers to each other at the park, we would watch our dogs play together and laugh at them. Zeke used his bulk to steamroll other dogs out of the way in his quest to be first. Often the target was three-month-old Paco. Zeke struck, Paco rolled defensively on his back (a signature move we later coined "the Dingo Roll"), and I apologized. Then I got a date. Fast forward a few years and we were married.

The dogs had unintentionally aligned our goals. What began as two strangers quickly became a team with common objectives: exercise the dogs and keep them out of trouble. Once we had a few common goals, many more (non-dog related ones) fell into place. We both were leaving intense

---

[35] Daft 2005
[36] Pierce and Newstrom 2008
[37] Burke 1966

relationships, and looking for something more laid back. Before long, we both had the common goal of creating new lives out of the wreckage of Hurricane Katrina.

The dog park has a great atmosphere. Plenty of dogless people show up just for the company. The swirling masses of animals makes everyone forget their problems and creates a light and carefree environment. For those few minutes a day at the dog park everyone just wants to unwind and enjoy watching all the activity. Everyone is aligned in purpose while they are at the park, whether they are aware of it or not.

Leaders also bring people together. They adjust the purpose and direction of other people's efforts. A director motivates her team to accomplish a common goal by the deadline. A spiritual leader aligns the intent and actions of his followers through inspiration. There's a lot of power in coordinating the efforts and intentions of others, which leaders tap into to create success. One useful way to conceptualize this comes from eighth grade math class: vectors. These little arrows have two characteristics: a direction and a magnitude. That is, they point in a certain direction, and they have a certain length. Both elements are easy to see:

## Vector A                    Vector B

Vector A points up and to the right and has a larger magnitude (length) than vector B. Vector B is directed straight down and has a smaller magnitude than vector A. Let's call vector A "Anne" and vector B "Bill":

## <u>Anne</u>                      <u>Bill</u>

Now let's pretend Anne and Bill work together on a project team. Each exerts individual effort toward the work, and each is motivated by different goals. Just from looking at the length of the two we can see that Anne puts in more effort at work than Bill does. Since her vector is about three to four times longer than his, we can say she's putting in three to four times as much effort in the office.

But vectors don't tell us much unless their direction means something. So let's say right and left represent how hard each person is working on the project as opposed to other projects. The more the vector points to the right, the harder the person is working on completing this project, and the more the vector points left, the more energy they are putting into other projects. Up and down represent motivation. The more the vector points up, the greater the person is motivated by money. The vector pointing down indicates motivation by recognition and promotion. The magnitude (length) of the vector represents how hard they are working in general. The longer the vector, the harder they are working. The background, or vertical and horizontal axes, would look like this:

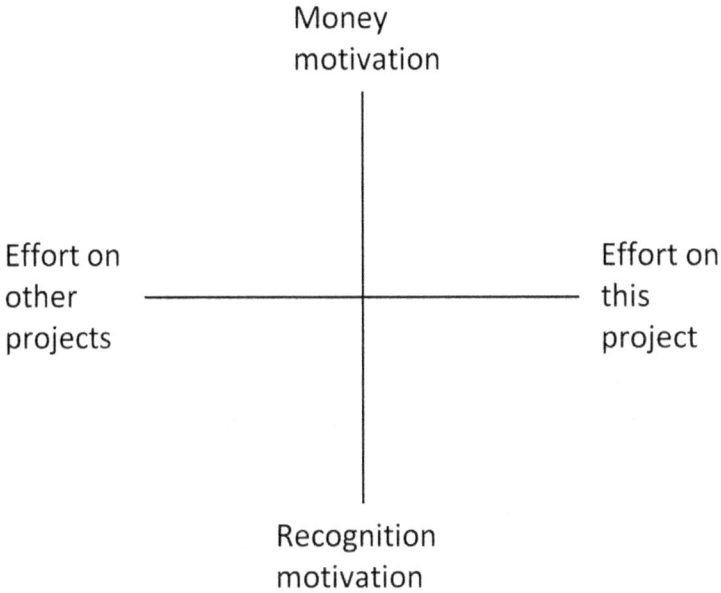

In order to arrive at what an individual person's vector would look like, they would be asked to rate themselves on the two dimensions above on a scale of –5 to 5:

*Effort*

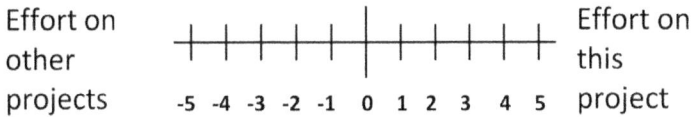

*Motivation*

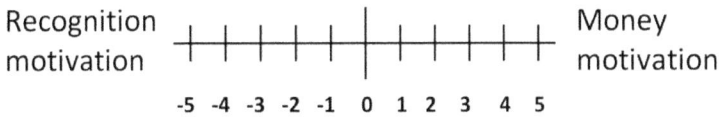

Their responses are then plotted to make their unique vector.

Now we take each person's vector and place it on the axes:

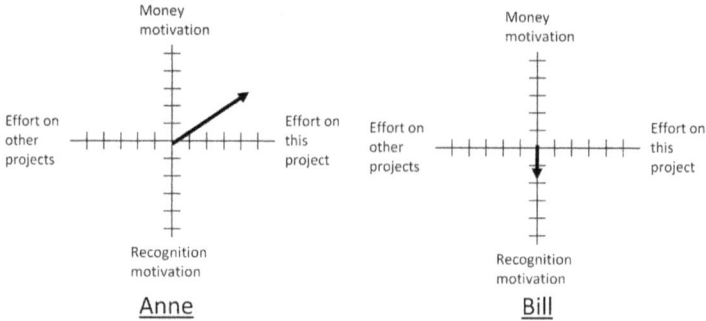

Anne

Bill

Anne is motivated about 70 percent by money and is spending about 80 percent of her effort on this group project in relation to other demands for her time.[38] Bill, on the other hand, splits his time equally between this and other projects, and is motivated by recognition alone. Since Anne's vector is longer, we can see that she's exerting more effort overall than Bill.

How could we gauge the collective team effort? Think back to geometry class again. The way to add vectors is to place them end to end and draw a new vector from the beginning of the first vector to the end of the last one. We place Bill's vector on the end of Anne's, and then draw a (dashed) line to indicate the combined team vector:

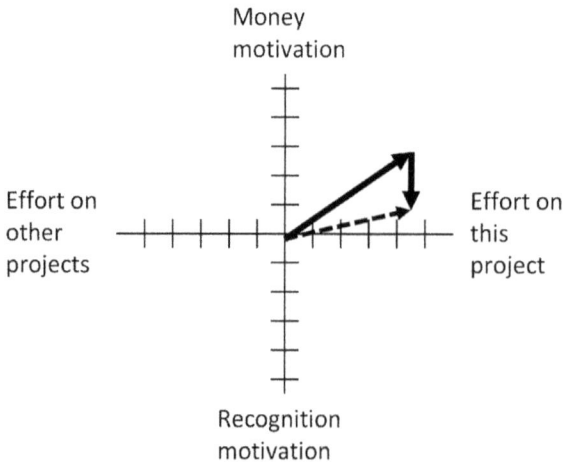

[38] These numbers are just guessed roughly. If Anne's vector was positioned at exactly a 45° angle above the x-axis, then she would be motivated 75% by money and 25% by recognition.

The team vector incorporates the magnitude and direction of each individual component, and is a good indication of how it's performing. To examine it more closely, remove the individual vectors:

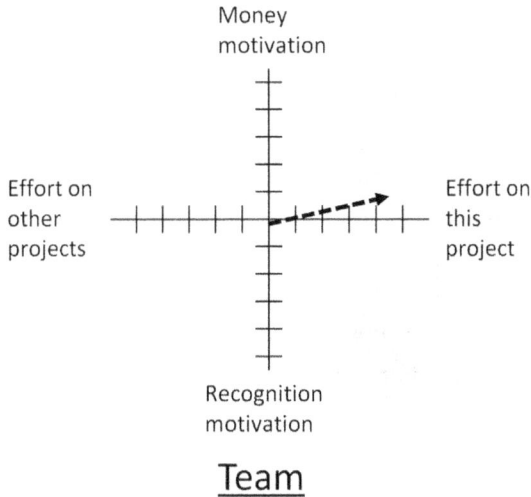

Money
motivation

Effort on
other
projects

Effort on
this
project

Recognition
motivation

## Team

Are the members working toward the project goals? To what extent? Are they motivated more by money or by recognition? Anne and Bill's team seems to be working about 90 percent on this project over others, and motivated by money a little more than recognition (about 60 percent/40 percent). How hard are they working in general (total effort while in the office)? This can be determined by the length of the team vector:

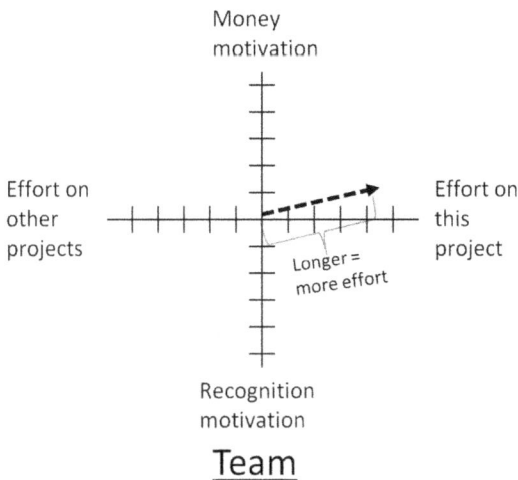

Money
motivation

Effort on
other
projects

Effort on
this
project

Longer =
more effort

Recognition
motivation

## Team

With this information their manager, Claire, has a better idea not only where they stand but how to make them more productive. She can tell Anne and Bill that this project will bring them recognition in the form of a promotion and raise, if completed successfully and on time. In this way she's actively aligning their efforts (their vectors). The manager may also pull Bill aside and tell him that the vice president is keeping a close eye on this particular project, and success here would be good for his career. This should encourage Bill to spend more time on this versus other competing work.

To determine what impact Claire's efforts had on the progress of the team, she again assesses the position of each member using vectors. Note that they still have the same motivations, as Bill's arrow is still as "tall" as it was toward recognition, and Anne's is still as "tall" as it was toward money. But now the model indicates that each one is working more on this project, and exerting more effort in general:

To see how much the team effort has changed, the vectors are again added up:

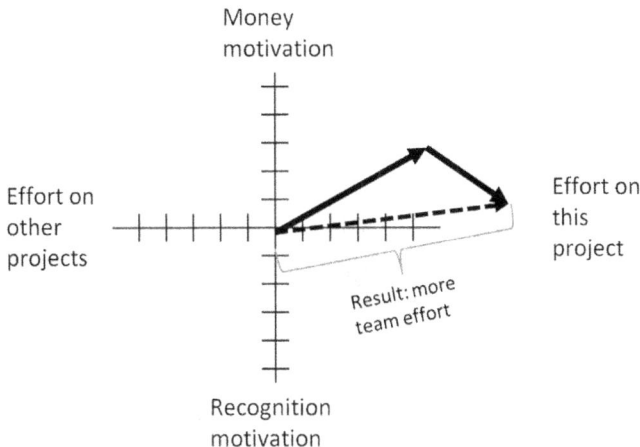

Money
motivation

Effort on
other
projects

Effort on
this
project

Result: more
team effort

Recognition
motivation

## Team after Claire's Actions

Now the length of the dashed line is longer and more directly pointing to the right, indicating increased overall effort and more concentration on this over other projects. Claire can feel confident her intervention was sufficiently motivating. By putting the old team vector and the new one side by side, she can gauge just how successful she was:

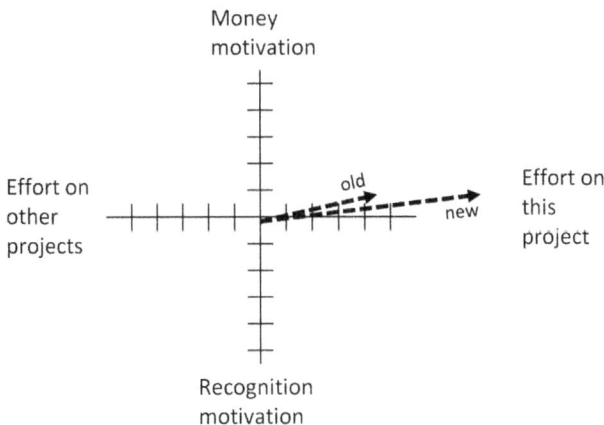

Money
motivation

Effort on
other
projects

old

new

Effort on
this
project

Recognition
motivation

## Comparing New and Old Team Vectors

The new vector looks about twice as long, so she could claim that she improved team effort by 100 percent. It almost lies directly on the x-axis toward "Effort on this project" so she can also let her boss know that her team is now devoting 8 percent more of their effort to this project (it used to be about 90 percent, now it's about 98 percent). If she measured more precisely using a grid (like graph paper), she could calculate exactly how much she improved the team. This "vector method" shows how leaders bring people together and align their goals to accomplish common goals. Leaders with more team members to manage can simply include more vectors to the model:

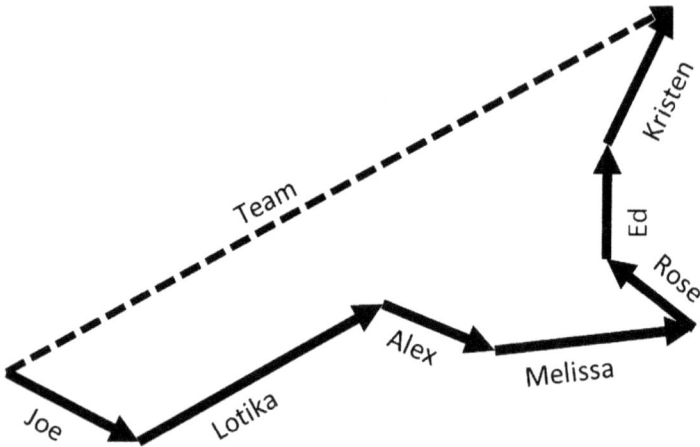

The takeaway is that leaders have many tools at their disposal to coordinate the efforts and successes of others toward ends that benefit the whole organization.[39] A group becomes a team with focused and directed effort toward a common end, and a good leader helps to provide that function.

---

[39] This concept will be developed more fully in an upcoming book

# Lesson

Leaders provide direction. Instead of simply focusing on controlling others in order to achieve results, they provide a broader meaningful context that answers the question of where everyone should be going and why. In the absence of this direction, everyone is left to determine for themselves how best to achieve common goals. Even that is assuming that (a) they know what those goals are and (b) they care about achieving them. Learn to think of your team members, or people you want to motivate, in terms of the vector method. Help to align them and bring them together to define, pursue, and accomplish common desired goals. Provide a broader meaning and shared culture and core values. The more you hone this skill, the greater the effectiveness of your leadership. Think of how the dogs at the park naturally align the interests and activities of their owners. Each dog motivates its owner out of what he was doing and toward the common interest of the park's activities (and to fulfill the dog's wishes to play).

# 15

To Adopt or Not?

*Learning how in-groups and out-groups work*

Poor Paco was almost given away weeks after my mother-in-law adopted him. When he was no bigger than a fat squirrel, she would try to pick him up from behind, startling him. His nascent defensive instincts would kick in, and he'd nip at her with his needle puppy teeth. Pancho, his brother, didn't have such tense nerves and would let himself be approached any which way.

Because of this aggressiveness, he developed a reputation. And since he had only been in the house a few weeks it was too early to see all of his positive qualities. At one point Kathy decided that she did not want a biting dog around and almost gave him up to "someone with more land, where he would be better suited." She didn't want Michaele to have him either. After all, who wants to hand off a biting animal to her daughter? Paco was given another chance and soon won everyone over with his endearing and infuriating personality. But it was close there for a while.

Kathy, as the leader of the pack, had approached both puppies with equal opportunity. Pancho responded favorably, while Paco was prickly and difficult. These first few interactions helped Kathy decide who was in her in-group (she kept Pancho) and who was in her out-group (she gave Paco to Michaele).

Whether they know it or not, leaders tend to segregate followers early on. Members of in-groups enjoy a closer relationship with the leader, more attractive work and assignments, and more recognition for their efforts. They also have higher satisfaction levels with their boss and experience less role-related stress (most likely as a result of the better assignments!). Simply put, in-group members get more attention and support from their leader.

Out-group members may tend to be viewed more as interchangeable commodities by the leader. They have more distant relationships with their boss and are usually assigned less challenging and less rewarding work. The relationship tends to be seen as distant and based on economic exchanges (you work, I pay you for it). These followers are more likely to have issues with their boss and may even file grievances. They certainly are less motivated to perform and report lower levels of job satisfaction.

As followers, we'd all like to be in the in-group, of course. And as leaders it would be great if our relationships with our followers were all high-quality, like those with our in-group members. So why would anyone want the out-group to exist?

According to Leader-Member Exchange (LMX) theory, people essentially self-sort into in- and out-group members early on. The first couple of interactions with your new boss are very important. Depending on how you respond to the first assignments and interactions as a follower, you are quickly steering yourself into either one group or another. You're defining your relationship going forward and essentially indicating which group you want to be in.

Here's how it works. As a leader makes requests to a member (or follower), that member responds in a certain way. He may either embrace the request and fulfill it to the best of his ability or take a lazy and shortcut approach. From this initial exchange a leader starts to form an impression of the member: *This guy is on the ball and delivers while this other guy doesn't.*

Usually the leader starts out slowly with small requests and then escalates their importance. By observing how well members respond, they are then segregated (consciously or unconsciously) into in-group and out-group members by the leader. Once those roles are formed, they are very hard to change. Every so often a leader may give an out-group member a chance to redeem herself and get back in, but this is not common.

In-group members are not only more satisfied in their work, but they have higher performance as well. They perceive that they are treated well for their efforts, so they are more motivated to perform. Out-group members feel like the cards are stacked against them. They are not motivated to work hard, because they feel that they'll always be on the outside. These people may work just hard enough to not get fired. They rationalize that if their only motivation is a paycheck (as opposed to attention and status of the in-group) then they will scale back their efforts to match that pay.

Research has shown that "those who had high-quality relationships with their immediate supervisor viewed the workplace as being more fair than those with low-quality relationships with their boss."[40] This makes sense. If you get along well with your boss, you see the office as fair. If you hate your boss, you don't. Zeke, who has proven himself stubborn and untrustworthy off the leash, probably considers it unfair that Paco runs free during most of our walks, while he remains restricted on the leash. Paco has been given a chance to be in the "in-group"—in this case the select status of being

---

[40] Scandura 1999

off leash—and has proven himself up to the responsibility. Therefore he is awarded a special status by his boss (me). No matter how many times I try to let Zeke off leash, he spoils the experience by running off, not coming when called, or generally getting in trouble. I get the "poor me" look from him when I tie his leash to a tree and he watches Paco chase after a Frisbee, free as a bird.

This also brings up the idea of trust. Increased levels of trust between a leader and follower have been shown to increase team performance, as it "allows the team to be willing to accept the leader's activities, goals, and decisions and work hard to achieve them."[41] Further, "trust in leadership allows team members to suspend their questions, doubts, and personal motives and instead throw themselves into working toward team goals."[42] I trust Paco off leash. Therefore, as a team, he and I are more productive at our common goal (going out to enjoy the day and use up some energy doing something fun). Since I don't trust Zeke off the leash, we are a less effective team at achieving that same goal. We end up going for shorter walks, using up less energy and having less overall enjoyment in the process.

As with all leadership theory, it is important to ask, "Ok, so what does this mean to me?" The lessons here are these:

- If you are a follower (employee, team member, etc): make sure that when you start a new job you make that extra effort in the first months. Be aware that your boss will be looking to see whether you are trustworthy, hardworking, and capable. This is your chance to get in the in-group, that inner circle that is close to the boss. If you have been at a job for a while, ask yourself which group you are in. If you are in the out-group, make efforts to approach the boss for more challenging and demanding work, and deliver when you get it. You may be able to fight your way in to the in-group after all. But remember that if you are not happy in your work, or you feel that you are not

[41] Dirks 2000
[42] ibid.

treated fairly, look at your own actions as well in the context of LMX theory and see if you had anything to do with your situation.

- If you lead others: be aware that you have an in-group and an out-group of followers. You may have noticed yourself psychologically, emotionally, or physically placing people in one or another. Maybe it happened unconsciously. There's nothing wrong with this as long as you frequently open your doors to the out-group and give them a chance to perform, allowing entry into the in-group. One example would be every three months choose a member of the out-group and give them a challenging assignment. If they step up to the challenge and excel, then consider bringing them into the fold. You want everyone to be in the in-group, as you will then be surrounded with capable, happy, and motivated people. Your leadership will be more effective as you work through this team.

# Lesson

Learn how in-groups and out-groups are formed. Whether you are the leader who decides, or the employee who is affected, the more prepared you are the better you can navigate them. Make an effort to have early wins with a new boss. Show effort and talent, but do so confidently and modestly. I made the decision to adopt Zeke in about five minutes after I met him. Don't be the dog in the out-group who is left behind in the shelter.

# 16

## Facebook for Dogs
### *Building a network your own way*

For a little while in my twenties I worked a job in "advertising." At least that's what the job posting said. I had just left Madison, Wisconsin, to reconnect with my family and friends on the East Coast and was back at my parents' house in Massachusetts looking for a job. Not only had I found this great listing describing a position in advertising with unlimited potential for a motivated individual, but I had landed an interview and then a job offer within a week! I was flying high, confident that finally my talents had been recognized and ready to explore the sexy world of corporate advertising (and this was before *Mad Men*!).

Turns out, it was door-to-door sales. My visions of grandeur instantane-ously evaporated and my ego got bruised, but I decided to give it a shot. My new coworkers were friendly, young, and energetic, and besides, it was a job and the earning potential did exist. The daily routine was this: receive a map highlighting a new territory, knock on a hundred doors, and come back to those same houses three times before nightfall to retry houses where the person was just out (or more likely, ducking you). If someone opened the door, try like hell to sell them a coupon book for local businesses for twenty bucks, half of which was your commission. Every single day. Rain or shine. Good neighborhood or bad. It was tough.[43]

On a good day you might make two hundred dollars, but bad days meant coming home empty handed and demotivated. For me it was a real study in force of will and positive mood. The rule of thumb was that you would get nine rejections for every one person who said yes. And of those nine rejec-tions—let me tell you—at least three were not friendly in the *least*. I even had a guy pull a gun on me right at his front door. Apparently his wife had spotted all six feet four inches of me coming up the driveway at dusk and didn't remember inviting anyone over.[44] Going to the next door after that one with a smile on my face took some real intestinal fortitude.

I quit after three months, which translates into roughly six thousand knocks on a stranger's door to sell them something. The benefits of the job were unforeseen, unintended, and long lasting. My skin was thicker and any trepidation I had about talking to people I didn't know was gone. Interestingly, my opinion of low-income neighborhood residents rose (much friendlier people) and my opinion of residents in high-income neighborhoods

---

[43] There were some cool little psychological tricks they taught us. Apparently if you get people to say the word "yes" many times in a row by answering simple questions, it is harder for them to say "no" when you ask them to purchase. Also, if you put an item in someone's hand, then snatch it back from them, and repeat the process a few times, apparently the person gets possessive and wants the item for himself (and wants you to stop taking it away!)

[44] I tried to adjust to people's surprise at seeing a huge stranger at their door by wearing a fluores-cent orange jacket, thinking maybe it would be less threatening. It might have just confused them more—who wears such an annoyingly bright jacket over a dress shirt, tie, and slacks?

fell (this is where I had the gun pulled on me—surprise!). I also discovered that the one-in-ten rule actually turned out to be true. Of every ten people I talked to, I had roughly one sale. This stuck with me, and I began to see its application in other situations.

So what does this have to do with leadership, the dogs, or building networks? Years later, when I was happily *not* knocking on a hundred doors a day, I started noticing Zeke and Paco as they met new people, whether at the park, in our house, or during a walk. Zeke loves everybody and runs right up to strangers. Within seconds he's in their lap or getting a free back scratch. Michaele and I joke that he's the flirt, while Paco plays hard to get. Paco is a one- or two-person dog. He takes forever to approach anybody new with any friendliness. At the park new people are treated as if they are trees; they're just inanimate objects for him to dodge as he races after the ball. At home, he's likely to greet a new acquaintance with a backward glance as he runs for the back room marking his exit with a trail of pee.

The typical dog park denizen loves most animals, meaning Zeke's befriending of them in minutes isn't much of an accomplishment. However, his gregariousness and genuine love for everybody is so infectious that he manages to make lots of new friends simply walking down the street. His accomplishments in this regard are even more impressive when you consider he's a mutt with a lot of pit bull in him. If there's any dog who doesn't get the benefit of doubt when encountered on the street, it's a dog that looks like a pit bull.[45] Despite this, he manages to convert many people to his side, many more than one in ten. They are his ever-expanding network.

Paco, on the other hand, has made maybe three new friends in the last five years. He simply has no interest in new people, and it shows. Sometimes we broach the subject of what would happen to the dogs if for whatever

---

[45] I've had people literally cross the street to avoid him and then cross back afterwards. So sad. If they only knew Paco was the nipper.

reason we couldn't keep them anymore.[46] When the subject comes up as to who might adopt them, Zeke's list is endless. Many have said, upon knowing Zeke for only a day or two, "Boy, if you ever need a home for him let me know—I would love to take him!" And then there's poor Paco. Michaele's father would take him in a heartbeat. My college roommate prefers him over dopey Zeke. Oh, and there's a rancher we know outside of Houston who would use him to herd his cattle.[47]

Paco has no network, while Zeke's is huge. It's all about options. Leadership deals with influence, opening up opportunities and making connections. All of these involve knowing a wide range of people whose expertise, connections, and goodwill can be drawn on.[48] In addition, the larger your network, the more new information you learn and the more accurate and useful your resulting mental models.[49] When the word "network" comes up, it can be intimidating. The image arises of powerful people who can call on thousands of others for favors. Maybe we think of the LinkedIn member with the coveted "500+ connections" status. But it doesn't have to be this overwhelming or complex. A good network may consist of only a dozen people who know you, respect you, and are willing to help out when needed. Many people in smaller towns in America have better networks than city dwellers, which seems counterintuitive. We may think of someone in the city as immersed in connections, expanding their network every day. But how many of these could be called on in a time of need? Would they present new opportunities and help the person use influence? In many cases, they wouldn't, while the resident of a small town may have a handful of lifelong relationships that would fulfill these needs and more.

---

[46] I should point out that this is unlikely, as we have found ways to bring them along while living and traveling on the West, East, and Gulf coasts and across a dozen countries in Europe.

[47] In fact, it was Gary's ranch we evacuated to after Hurricane Katrina. He liked Paco so much he went out and got his own blue heeler, a laid-back herder he named Fred. Fred's cool.

[48] Another important lesson: everyone expects to be paid back. You grow your network by being of value to others.

[49] See chapter 7, "OK, Now This," for more information on mental models.

In this sense Paco is building his network in a different way. He may only have a few people whom he can call on, but every one of them would adopt him if needed, and give him whatever he needs. There's a deep sense of loyalty and commitment. Zeke's network is huge, but a smaller percentage would actually be there for him when it counts. He's like the Facebook girl with four hundred "friends" of which only forty could be considered a friend in real life. Paco is the Luddite who shuns social media, instead choosing to invest heavily in a few real friends.

# Lesson

Better networks make for better leaders. Networks increase a leader's access to power and influence, and provide a constant source of new information that challenges outmoded and inefficient mental models. There is no right way to build a network. Zeke shows that the "shotgun" approach works, and that if you are genuinely interested in people and approach them regularly, you will build a decent network without too much additional effort. This can then be drawn upon for new opportunities and influence. But you may find the one-in-ten rule applies: only 10 percent may be there if you really need them. The other approach is to invest heavily in a small network. Those in this network may be more loyal and reliable, but they are much fewer in number. This limits your scope of influence and opportunity. Which is right? Only you can decide where on this spectrum you feel comfortable. Either way building and maintaining a network is an important component to exercising leadership skills.

# 17

Following like a Lost Puppy

*The importance of a first follower*

The irony is not lost on me that I'm writing a leadership book on nature's perfect follower: the dog. They have faith in you as their owner and often show love and enthusiasm for whatever you decide the two of you should do. Go for a walk in a downpour? *Great idea! Let's go!* Time for bed? *Perfect! Let's go!* One of the seemingly endlessly forwarded e-mails for animal aficionados is a comparison of the diary of a dog to that of a cat. The cat writes of torment and his efforts to outwit his captors, while the dog's diary reads:

8:00 a.m.     Dog food! My favorite thing!

9:30 a.m.     A car ride! My favorite thing!

9:40 a.m.   A walk in the park! My favorite thing!

10:30 a.m.   Got rubbed and petted! My favorite thing!

12:00 p.m.   Lunch! My favorite thing!

1:00 p.m.   Played in the yard! My favorite thing!

3:00 p.m.   Wagged my tail! My favorite thing!

5:00 p.m.   Milk bones! My favorite thing!

7:00 p.m.   Got to play ball! My favorite thing!

8:00 p.m.   Wow! Watched TV with the people! My favorite thing!

11:00 p.m.   Sleeping on the bed! My favorite thing![50]

What does this ideal follower role teach us about leadership? A leader is nothing without his first follower.

In a recent TED talk, Derik Sivers spoke about how to start a movement.[51] He showed video footage of an outdoor concert in which there was one person, apparently moved by the music and perhaps a few drinks, dancing all by himself in a clearing on the field. The dance was unconventional, with the sole carefree dancer there jerking around and having the time of his life. The videographer clearly wanted to document this crazy person so that he could laugh with friends about him later. Then an interesting thing happened. A second person walked into the clearing and started dancing in the same wacky way the first guy was. In no more than a few minutes, a third and fourth person joined, and within five minutes there was a jubilant crowd of more than twenty people all dancing the same funky dance and living it up. This guy started a movement. But it wasn't the original dancer who made the movement happen—it was the second one, the one I'll call the first follower.

---

[50] This version is found at http://www.animaltalk.us/excerpts-from-a-dog-and-a-cat-diary/
[51] Sivers 2010; TED.com is a great resource for videos of talks on almost any subject, free of charge.

As Sivers points out, the second guy on the scene gave the initial dancer credibility. He sent the message that he believed in what this unusual guy was trying to do, and by joining him, started to provide legitimacy in the eyes of onlookers. *Maybe that guy isn't crazy—there's someone else dancing his funky dance.* This first follower lowered the social barriers to joining and made it less risky for others to get up and groove. *That looks like fun—maybe I should try it.* Of course, as more and more joined, the risks fell even more, to the point where it was more socially acceptable to be part of the dancing mob than to be sitting out. *I better get out there and dance or people are going to think I'm a loser!*

It struck me that this is exactly what my dogs do for me. They are the ideal first followers because they give their wholehearted enthusiastic support to almost any crazy idea I have. If I feel like rolling around on the floor with them and playing tug-of-war with a blanket, they're all in. Imagine what I would look like if they just sat in the corner eying me suspiciously as I tried to entice them to play by dangling a blanket around. Once they participate, even the most serious observer should accept that I'm just a guy romping around with his dogs.

Consider eating at a café by yourself. While more accepted in Europe, it's still unusual to see someone dining by themselves in the United States. Now change one element—imagine you have a dog under your chair, leash wrapped around the legs of the table. All of a sudden you're more accepted. The dog is the universal first follower, a reliable go-to enthusiastic supporter who lends an air of leadership to the otherwise lone person.

This is an important point. Typically the image of a leader is one who does not need the support of others; he breaks forth and charts his own path. But what is a leader without followers? Who is the entrepreneur without the first person to believe in her product, whether it happens to be a venture capitalist or an end consumer? Without that first follower she's just a person with a lot of ideas—that person dancing out there in the field by herself. It's the first follower who starts to provide traction for the initial pioneer. This starts the movement that propels that person into a leadership role.

A leadership scholar concluded that:

> The follower is always there when leadership occurs. It is he who accepts or rejects leadership. It is he who follows reluctantly or enthusiastically, obediently or creatively. In any situation where leadership occurs, he is there with all of his psychological attributes. He brings with him his habits, attitudes, preferences, biases, and deep-lying psychological needs.[52]

Not only does a follower bring a lot to the leader-follower relationship, she may enable the leader to actually *be* a leader *at all*. A follower carries around a prototype of a perfect leader in her head and compares what she sees against that ideal.[53] Is he as smart as her conception of a leader? As tall? As capable? As authoritative (or lenient)? The extent of the "fit" between the two determines whether she considers the person a leader at all. In many ways, she (along with other followers) grants the "leader" his status as such. Have you ever been in a group where one person really wants to be the leader, yet can't be because no one else allows him to? It's a subtle dance where the would-be leader's efforts become increasingly obvious and desperate as the group collectively ignores, downplays, and diffuses them. Usually social etiquette keeps them from simply saying, *You're not leader material. We don't want to be led by you.* But usually the message gets across anyhow.

My wife, who is interested in sustainable development, happened across the Guerrilla Gardener[54] online not too long ago. He's a man who decided to take unused public spaces—even as small as dirt patches in between sidewalks—and turn them into something useful and beautiful. Edible and

---

[52] Hollander 1992
[53] ibid.
[54] http://www.guerrillagardening.org/

beautiful plants are surreptitiously planted to transform the neglected to the beautiful. He was the first to realize that there was unused and unkempt public space that could be put to better use and blog about it. Through the Internet he got his first follower, then his second, and so on. The idea spread all over the world. Now he states that if you're interested in doing a little guerilla gardening of your own, you should first post a place and time you will be there on his site, and you will most likely have a dozen people show up to help you. In a sense, he has created a platform for other people to find their own first followers for their guerilla gardening project. There are even paying advertisers displaying banners for "guerilla gardening tools." Imagine if he never had his first follower. He would be "that guy" in the neighborhood who is always digging around in dirt by the road and planting things. You might look at him out your window and say "Hey honey, there he is again planting tomatoes by the curb." Instead, he has started a movement and is seen as its legitimate leader.

My mother is a retired middle school librarian. During her coursework for her master's, she took a reference course which covered all kinds of publications, some of them quite odd. She discovered that there was a magazine dedicated entirely to collectors of antique barbed wire. Can you imagine the first person to start collecting antique barbed wire? Where would he (or she) be without that second person who said, "You know what, I like antique barbed wire too!"

The takeaway here is that if you have an entrepreneurial spirit, or otherwise like to take charge and do your own thing, it is important to keep in mind that you should be looking for your first follower. That first follower may help you turn your singular (and sometimes peculiar) passion into a movement, with you as the leader. It's OK to start out with your dog as your first follower, but eventually you may want to move on to people. Try the Internet—there seems there are all kinds of people out there...and you never know who your first follower might be!

# Lesson

Dogs are natural first followers. If you want to be a leader, have the guts to put yourself out there. Keep an eye out for your first follower, the person who believes in what you are doing—who sees the vision—and who through their commitment can give you the traction to become a leader of your own movement. Do what you can to encourage followers. If you believe in what someone else is doing, don't be afraid to be their first follower.

# 18

The Dog Park Ambassador
*Relationship building*

Leadership involves regular interaction with other people. In fact, one of a leader's central functions is relationship building. From this foundation stems motivation, influence, empowerment, communication, and alignment. There are books full of stories about leaders who memorized the name of everyone they met and remembered at least one thing about each so they could make a connection later. Leaders have to delegate, manage, and work through others to get things done. That means dealing with many personalities—which isn't always so easy.

No matter who you are and what you do for a living, there are people with whom you must work with. If you get along with them, they can make your life a little easier. This chapter, however, isn't so much about interacting with those whom you already know. It's about the state of mind of a leader upon meeting someone for the first time and setting the tone. Whether it be networking, establishing a new working relationship, creating an opportunity, closing a deal, or simply interacting with others, leaders need to know how to work with new people.

Many times over the years I've noticed how people I've met surface again and again in different contexts. I may meet a person at an event who is a friend of a friend. A year passes with no further contact, and suddenly they are sitting across the table from me closing a deal. There are many non-work related examples as well: the mom on the sidelines at your daughter's soccer game may be the one sitting next to you at the next PTA meeting, or the mechanic who fixes your car may be the one coaching your son's little league baseball team. A friend of mine took a new job and happened to mention to his mother the name of his new boss. It turns out she knew him—it was the guy who sat next to her six years earlier at a high school football game, screaming at his son.

So far none of this should be surprising. We all know that it's a small world and you shouldn't burn bridges. The key here is that the effective leaders I've observed all employ a certain approach when they meet new people. This mindset maximizes the potential for future opportunities, and helps to prevent future awkward situations and potential difficult situations. Zeke seems to be a natural at it.

Going to the dog park is like opening up Forrest Gump's box of chocolates—you never know just what you're going to get. You may be alone with your dog throwing the ball without fear of it being snagged by a hoarding hound, or it may be packed with dozens of dogs and owners milling around. At the park in Belgium there was the occasional scruffy outcast passed out by the tree line surrounded by empty beer cans or some young travelers setting up an illegal tent for a free night's stay. This can make for some stressful times if your dog is off leash and you aren't sure how they are going to react.

Paco tends to be focused on us and the Frisbee, but Zeke is always "the park ambassador." He roams around from person to person and dog to dog, sizing everyone up and greeting them like he owns the place.

Whether he approaches another dog or is approached by it, he always starts off in a very open manner. Tail up, head up, casual and calm, he'll encounter each one with no prejudgments or biases. After a few quick sniffs he's concluded that he either likes and is interested in them, or is not. New friends are unconditionally accepted, and he turns on the charm. They are best friends within minutes. It's amazing.

When he gets the wrong vibe, he simply moves on. He doesn't run away, lunge at them and snarl, or even stand up tall to prove he's dominant. He just politely moves on over to the next dog or an interesting-smelling patch of ground. What's interesting is that he doesn't display any aggressive body language. Friends are embraced, others get a quick glance, and he's on his way.

Think back to the last time you were in a social situation where you realized you didn't like the person you just met. Maybe it was at a party or in another department with a coworker. How did you react? Did you squirm and look uncomfortable? Maybe you made a dismissive comment to end the conversation? Plenty of people with status immediately decide that they are superior to their new acquaintance and make it clear right away with derisive behavior. In their eyes, it's OK to treat someone badly if they are not a friend.

However, some of the most effective leaders, no matter how much money or status they have, are humble and open. They realize that every person they meet deserves basic respect. Even if you aren't interested in talking any longer there's no need to do anything other than politely move on. This isn't to say that these leaders enjoy everyone's company or have to pretend that they do. It's simply that those who exhibit leadership skills know how to skillfully and respectfully navigate their way socially. The uninteresting person today might be the decision maker in an important deal tomorrow. By creating only good or neutral impressions, all doors stay open for future interaction.

Approaching situations, social and otherwise, with an open mind can open new opportunities as well. Leaders recognize that frankness and candor in new situations and with new people can lead to creative and innovative outcomes, whether it's a solution to an existing problem or a new line of business.

# Lesson

Leaders approach social situations with an open mind and don't pre-judge. Once they have gotten an impression of someone, they either embrace them wholeheartedly or politely move on. Focus on making at best a positive impression and at worst a neutral one. Avoid fake friendliness (most people can easily see through it) but it is important to treat everyone like they may be important at some point in your future.

# 19

# Bad Dog!
## *Using negative feedback to your advantage*

**W**hether you lead or are led, feedback is an important part of development. How can you know whether you are progressing toward your goal if you don't have a candid assessment of where you are right now? It would be like using a GPS that doesn't want to hurt your feelings so it constantly tells you you're on track no matter which way you're driving. How would ever reach your destination?

Several models exist for using feedback for developmental purposes. For our purposes I'll choose one focused on followers and one on leaders, although in essence they are the same. Mary Mavis outlined a four-step process for giving "painless performance evaluations".[55]

---

[55] Mavis 1994

1. Observation → 2. Assessment → 3. Consequences → 4. Development → (repeat)

Through observation a problem is identified (employee is repeatedly late for work) and the situation is assessed (employee has poor time management skills). The consequences of the problem (actual or likely) are then considered, and then actions are taken to address it (a sit-down talk with the employee, a written warning, etc). Then the process begins again to evaluate whether the development efforts were successful, or if another approach needs to be taken. Another way to look at it is:

1. What's wrong? → 2. Why's it happening? → 3. What happens if things don't change? → 4. Actions taken to prevent recurrence of the problem. → (repeat)

The model for leadership development[56] is very similar, but adds support and removes the consequences step:

1. Assessment → 2. Challenge → 3. Support → (repeat)

This model is provided for those looking to develop leaders, such as executive coaches. The first step, assessment, consists of information gathered from various sources (from surveys to interviews to objective data on reports) to establish where the leader currently stands on any number of criteria (performance, likeability, etc). Where do their strengths lie? Their weaknesses? From there a challenge is issued to the leader to address areas of improvement so that they can reach the next level. Challenge can be provided in the form of "novelty [introduction to new experiences], difficult goals, conflict, and dealing with adversity" (ibid.). Support is then provided as appropriate. Each person may need support in a different way, but traditional methods include listening, feedback, and encouragement by a caring professional and personal network of people.

---

[56] Van Velsor, McCauley and Ruderman 2010

Feedback is not always welcome. I've set up and implemented annual review systems with many clients, and usually no one is thrilled about hearing from others about how they are doing. Everyone hopes for positive news, but we all dread hearing that there are areas where we need work. However, it's the negative feedback that's much more useful.

I've been told that a true friend is one who isn't afraid to give you honest critical feedback. It's rare to find someone close to us who cares enough to go through the awkwardness of giving constructive criticism. While not fun to deliver, and certainly not fun to receive, it is essential to growth. Pema Chodron, the Buddhist nun and author, compares the difficulties that life throws you to manure.[57] You can either curse your luck and constantly step around the pile or you can use it to cultivate and grow a beautiful garden.

Many of us have a tendency to ignore, reject, or make excuses when we get negative feedback. *It isn't my fault. I had no control. It was all because of someone else; why should I listen to his feedback? He's a jerk anyway.* And then there are those of us that obsess over negative feedback. We hear it, chew on it, internalize it, and use it as proof that all of our worries and insecurities are true: *I'm a failure—she even said so. I knew I was horrible at presenting. Maybe I shouldn't even try.*

The key to turning the dung of negative feedback into fertilizer for growth and development is to approach it wholly and openly, without judgment, and truly listen to what is being said. Make a mental note of it, and then move on. Zeke does this perfectly.

When we lived in San Francisco it was the first time that we had to leave the dogs alone for more than a few hours. At times, with both of us out of the apartment at either work or school, the dogs would be at home for hours at a time. Every so often they would decide that they had been left just a little too long and would show us just how displeased they were. They never went

---

[57] Chodron 1994

to the bathroom in the house, but Zeke had a unique way of expressing his unhappiness toward us.

We would come home to find one pillow completely obliterated. No other items were touched, moved, or damaged. The one he did choose for demise would be torn open, eviscerated, and ripped into almost identically sized small squares. The stuffing—along with the small squares of cover material—was separated into pieces about the size of a large cotton ball which were evenly distributed across the entire floor with almost geometric precision. The first few times I saw it I would have been more upset had I not been so impressed with his ability to place a grid of detritus perfectly across available floor space.

From the moment I opened the door on these few occasions Zeke would look stricken, ears back and wide-eyed with a long face, waiting for the hammer to fall. When I scolded him, which I suppose could be called "negative feedback," he put his head down, took the scolding seriously, and then quietly looked guilty until I uttered the word "OK." At that moment, like I had absolved him of all of his sins, he would snap fully back to his normal, happy, dopey self.

What's important is that he accepted the feedback without responding too much at the time. He didn't try to run away or fight back but simply accepted it and then, when it was over, moved past the whole event. Eventually he got the message that this wasn't acceptable, and I learned not to leave him alone for quite so long.

Of course we humans don't usually get this verbal release from our critics, so we need to develop an internal "Ok" that releases us from dwelling and obsessing on the criticism. After we hear the feedback, fully listen to it and try to refrain from an immediate response, we can later tell ourselves "Ok" and move on.

# Lesson

Learning how to receive negative feedback is an important skill. The tendency is to either respond with anger, denial, and excuses or to excessively internalize and dwell on the feedback. Neither of these reactions allows us to take the point of the message seriously and move on to use for self-improvement. Look for the valuable message in the feedback, consider it with perspective, and then put it aside.

# 20

꣠꣠

# Owners Are Friends
# with Money

*The importance of resources and contacts*

In one of my leadership courses at Boston University, I studied a case about the lives of several civil rights pioneers. These individuals, all of whom had made significant contributions toward their cause, had come from impoverished childhoods and meager beginnings. What they developed first, after a passion for learning, was a network. Even though they had few resources themselves, they met people who had wealth in the form of contacts and money. Since these future civil rights leaders had passion, charisma, and conviction, they were able to attract contacts and friends with money who supported them in their efforts.

After discussing the case in class, I came home and opened the door to my two rambunctious, silly, and at times annoying dogs. It struck me that they were living a good life—while of course not making a dime—simply because they had contacts with money (me and my wife) who found them compelling and endearing. They live on charisma alone, and we take care of the rest. Michaele and I sometimes joke about them "earning their keep" by protecting the house and how if we need extra income we could always rent Paco out to herd cattle part-time. But the truth of it is that they provide companionship, humor, and all the other perks of a loyal canine. Of course they don't need money.

It got me thinking about how many of us curb our aspirations or lower our expectations because of the perceived limitations of money. It may be that we go to a local state school because the desired private school we were admitted to is too expensive. Maybe we forgo college altogether. Or we think we can't ever leave our soul-numbing cubicle job to pursue what we love because we need the paycheck. Of course there are times when money is a real and important restriction, and we need to take it into consideration in our decisions. Unfortunately in too many cases it can end up being our go-to excuse, a crutch that we lean on to justify why we do not pursue another path that might make us happier. No risk, no reward, after all.

Entrepreneurs are known for their go-for-broke approach to following their passions. They don't let lack of money stand in the way of what they want to do. By following their passion, and finding ways to make it work financially afterwards, they tend to have good rates of success. Not every attempt will be successful, but out of the ashes of one attempt they will strive for their next one.[58] The first company may be funded on a credit card, or with money raised by friends and family, but once they are on their second and third companies they may have gotten the attention of other professional investors like venture capitalists. They may not have money themselves,

---

[58] I've heard that to be a successful entrepreneur you need to be a little bit crazy. Your drive has to outweigh your rationality.

but their charisma, drive, and passion become clear to their supporters with money, which leads to the success of all.

It's important to keep this in mind as we pursue our passions. Money may be an important factor, but it is not necessarily the most important factor that contributes to our success. Natural leaders follow their passions with a passing consideration for money but do not consider lack of money as an excuse to quit or to abandon their dreams for a steady paycheck.

# Lesson

**While money always makes things a little easier, it's OK to have little money and few resources as long as you have strong motivation, are compelling and have contacts who will help support your efforts with resources. If they believe in you, they will support you one way or another. Of course you don't want to depend solely on others, but for those first crucial steps to success use the resources you have.[59] I often look at the dogs and think what a sweet deal they have—nothing to do but play, eat and sleep. They don't make a dime but their enthusiasm, warmth, unconditional love, and drive provide pleasure to us, so we enjoy supporting them.**

---

[59] Ethically, of course. See the chapter on The Dog Park Ambassador. Besides simply being a decent human being, it's important to treat people well because you never know when people resurface in your life.

# 21

## Quietly the Best
### *Balancing self-confidence with humility*

Henry Ford once said, "Whether you believe you can, or you can't, you are right."[60]

One of the first traits of leaders identified was self-confidence. It's the basis of all other leadership skills. Without it, the chances of mastering any new skill are slim. After all, if you aren't confident in yourself, who else will be confident in you?

Self-confidence can be roughly defined as having the mettle to assume that through your actions you will be able to influence external events toward

---

[60] Ford 1937

a desired outcome. It's saying, "It can be done, and I can contribute toward that end." But it can be taken too far. It can also be based on false assumptions. Authentic and effective self-confidence relies on a realistic assessment of one's abilities and their effectiveness in a given situation. For instance, confidence that you can win the Boston Marathon without training and preparation is folly. It's based on an unrealistic assessment of your skills (the basic ability to run) and how well they fit the demands of the task (assuming that knowing how to run means finishing over two dozen miles before everyone else).

Effective self-confidence also relies on delivery. Bombastic, over-the-top assuredness usually turns others off and comes across as obnoxious. In many cases it can also send the exact opposite message—that you are insecure and are overcompensating by trying too hard to appear confident. It is important to balance confidence with humility.

Exhibiting humility sends the message that you are aware of your limitations and can make mistakes. Share credit for positive feedback you receive. Understate your achievements in favor of praising your team's achievements, and you will contribute significantly to your effectiveness as a leader. Think of the difference between Sally Field, who accepted her Academy Award in 1984 by famously saying, "You like me! You really, really like me!"[61] and Dustin Hoffman, who stood at the same podium with his Oscar in 1979 and lamented the fact that such an award pitted many talented and worthy actors against each other.[62] While Field's response has become the subject of countless parodies for its gleeful self-importance, the understated Hoffman roused his "team"—his peers at the awards ceremony—to a tearful standing ovation with his self-deprecating speech. People are motivated by others who accomplish great things while maintaining dignity and selflessness.

In a previous chapter I mentioned Zeke's self confidence in learning how to swim. His ability to jump in the water and try his best showed that he

---

[61] Porrill, The Worst Academy Award speeches of all time 2010
[62] Porrill, The Best Academy Award speeches of all time 2010

was confident he would figure it out and that he would be successful (by not drowning). If he doubted his skills, he would never have attempted to swim. Paco's self confidence is apparent when he sprints after a ball. No matter the size, speed, and number of competitors, he's certain that he'll be the one bringing back the ball. And he does. But neither dog is obnoxious in their confidence. They have areas that they know where they cannot compete (Paco in swimming, Zeke in ball retrieval) and don't pretend that they do. Just because they excel at one task doesn't mean they assume they'll be masters at everything. In the end, they're just dogs who show a healthy level of humility while confidently going about their day.

# Lesson

Cultivate authentic self-confidence and balance it with humility. This will contribute to others seeing you as a leader in your field. Authentic self-confidence means that you realistically assess your skills (and those of your team) and their effectiveness in the given situation without excessive swagger or bombast. Recognize the achievements of all, even when you are the only one being praised. Temper this self-confidence with humility, understatement, and selflessness to be most effective.

# 22

$\xi$—$3$

# Puppy Dog Eyes
*Developing personal magnetism*

Someone with personal magnetism can be described as charming, likeable, and charismatic. Their attractive personality increases the chances they will be seen as a leader by others. Their followers are happy to be around them and therefore are more willing to work with, and be led by, them.

From the very beginning, humanity's relationship with dogs (or their ancestors) has been mutually beneficial. Domesticated wolves provided a level of protection to early man by alerting him to dangers, while the animals benefitted from easier access to food. The days of man as a nomad are long over, but the human-dog relationship remains stronger than ever. In fact, the dogs now receive many more benefits including shelter, medical care, and in some cases even health insurance![63]

Dogs clearly continue to provide other benefits for people besides protection, including companionship and comfort. But one factor may best explain why we continue to take dogs as pets: charisma and personal magnetism. Dogs are brimming with charisma from the feisty Pomeranian all the way to the drooping basset hound, and we humans are drawn to that personal (or canine) magnetism.

When I decided to adopt a dog from the Japonica Street pound in New Orleans, I entered the kennel with an open mind. Although I tend to prefer bully breeds,[64] I was open to any dog that caught my eye. Walking past each pen, the personality of the dog within it was almost immediately apparent. There were the scared ones, the shy ones, the over-excited ones, and the ones that appeared to have given up all hope. Although my heart went out to all of them, knowing that many were on their last days and needed to be adopted to survive, there was one that stood out from all the rest. He was a five-month-old pit bull mix, a lanky, coffee-colored little guy with a swagger in his step and a little crescent-shaped scar by his eye. He seemed relaxed and cool in demeanor. Not distant-cool but cool in the vein of Miles Davis. That kind of cool. I asked to see him, and he was brought out to a small open air courtyard. He seemed politely interested in me, but not overly so, and after sniffing and licking my hand he swaggered about sniffing patches of grass. I knew that this was my dog.

His magnetism hooked me from our first meeting, and because of it he got adopted only a few months before Hurricane Katrina hit (I hate to think what happened to the dogs that had not been adopted in time). Since then,

---

[63] I have to plead guilty on that last one. When we lived in San Francisco we had visions of the dogs running off the cliffs by the sea and thought pet insurance was the way to go. Visions of $5,000 surgeries made the $19 a month seem like a deal.

[64] Several breeds of dogs fall under the "bully breeds" category, including the American pit bull terrier, American Staffordshire terrier, bull terrier, Staffordshire bull terrier, miniature bull terrier, American bulldog, and English bulldog.

his personality continues to pay off for both of us. Walking this dog, who coincidentally never lost his swagger, was the surest way to meet girls. He was, and still is, a girl magnet. As I mentioned in the introduction, he helped me meet my wife, and now she says that even when she walks him she gets a lot of attention from women. His charisma and appeal have earned him a roof over his head, a healthy diet, and lots of attention and affection over the years.

Paco is no different. His appeal differs in that he's more tightly wound and alert, but his charm is no less effective. Due almost entirely to his personality, he got himself adopted, fed, and cared for his whole life. The dogs' charm is not something that just hooks you in the beginning; it's an ongoing (mostly successful) effort put forth to get what they want. Whether he is hamming it up to get his back scratched by a visitor or looking sad and pathetic so we will give him a treat, Zeke knows how to manipulate each situation to his benefit. Paco's efforts seem less deliberate. He relies more on his natural appeal and less on obvious tactics. No matter the approach, the link is clear between their charisma and the willingness of others to provide for them.

Personal magnetism, charisma, and passion are key factors to creating your own personal brand as well. The more appealing and beguiling you are, the more unique and attractive you are to others. It's a way to stand out from the crowd. To learn more about developing your own personal brand, refer to the chapter, "Rebranding a Pit Bull."

# Lesson

By developing your personal magnetism and charisma you can make more inspirational and effective appeals and motivate others to follow your lead.

# 23

## Treats or Shouts

*Fear-based leading versus love-based leading*

Some claim their dogs only respond to a fear-based training approach, while others swear that positive reinforcement yields the best results. Do you yell when your dog doesn't come running at your call or do you give him a treat when he does?

I have to admit that I have tended to use a combination of the two, but the longer I have Paco and Zeke the more time I spend on the love-based approach. It takes more patience, but it works. When they were just puppies, and going through training "boot camp," I perfected my stern voice and had them stopping in their tracks at my command. My mother-in-law even jokingly called me "the General" for a while. "But hey," I'd say to her, "it works, doesn't it?" And it did—for a while.

Eventually Zeke learned that he could ignore me the first three times and come running on the fourth with no consequences. Paco, the more obedient of the two, also stopped heeding my every command[65]. They still listened to Michaele, who would reward them with Bil-Jac liver treats for obedience. (By the way, if you don't know what Bil-Jac treats are, just know that our dogs respond to them as if they should be a controlled substance in the dog world—they are *that* addictive). She's a natural nurturer, so she's been an advocate of the love-based approach from day one.

The situation in the work world is not so different. Love-based leadership is harder to find and harder to practice yet much more effective. The majority of organizations are permeated with fear-based leadership, right down from the top. A "do it or else" vibe trickles down—verbally or otherwise—down through the ranks. But research suggests this approach really isn't all that effective. Yes, it may get some results but usually only exactly what is asked for, no more and no less. Fear-based motivation leads to employee performance at the bare minimum level required as not to get fired. Employees under these conditions tend to just meet the requirements but won't go any further. Why would they? Creativity, spontaneity, and drive for excellence are simply not there.

Consider the difference between the following two employees. The first is motivated by fear, the other by love. Imagine both are bakers. The fear-motivated employee performs because she feels it is important not to look bad in front of her boss. She doesn't want to embarrass herself or be shown-up by others. Baking bread is joyless to her, and she's relieved when it's over and she gets to go home. Contrast this with the love-motivated employee. He gets completely absorbed by his work, and it leaves him feeling energized. Because he enjoys the experience, time flies by and his days seem pleasant and

---

[65] Part of this has to do with having two dogs. Training one dog is so much easier as they don't have another bad influence always by their side.

short. He's completely focused on the task at hand. Whose bread would you rather be eating?[66]

Fear-based leadership produces several negative side effects. It creates a culture of avoidance, where everyone is focused on staving off the bad, but no one is directed toward getting the good. In this type of culture mistakes aren't pointed out (for fear of punishment), ideas aren't offered (for fear of ridicule), and innovation is stifled (for fear of failure). There is no growth, only stagnation. Communication is poor, and there may be lots of office politics as people deflect punishment and negative consequences to others.

A love-based leadership style creates the opposite. There is a culture of participation, excitement, and passion. People contribute to meet and exceed requirements and achieve excellence because they love what they do and it makes them feel good. Mistakes still happen, but they are viewed as learning experiences. This encourages everyone to confront and correct them. Failures aren't the end of the world. Communication levels are high, problems are uncovered, and innovation and creativity drive the organization to new levels of competitiveness.

These principles apply not just with dogs and with corporate environments, of course, but across all human interactions. Love-based family relations are vastly preferable to fear-based ones. Friendships and social interactions produce many more positive effects without an undercurrent of punishment. By working toward love-based motivation, you are working with the energy that allows people to feel alive, happy, creative, connected, content, and satisfied.

It is a *pulling* motivation. It internally compels people though inspiration and enjoyment toward excellence. Fear-based motivation *pushes*. It propels people away from punishment and pain. When people are motivated toward something, it's easy to identify where they want to be. Leaders can then better align their efforts, knowing that they all are working toward the same

[66] Adapted from Daft 2005

goal. When people run away from pain, that same leader only knows where they *won't* be, not where they'll end up. This makes coordinating their efforts toward a common goal much more difficult. Think of a dog on the end of a leash. Isn't it easier to guide them with it by pulling rather than pushing? Eisenhower famously said, "Pull the string, and it will follow wherever you wish. Push it, and it will go nowhere at all."[67]

---

[67] Eisenhower n.d.

# Lesson

Fear-based approaches get some minimal or temporary results, but ultimately they will fail. Love-based motivation and love-based leadership inspire the mind, heart, talents, and passions of others and pull them toward excellence. Throw that stick away, and go buy a bag of carrots.

# III

# Reading Others

This section examines how working through others becomes more effective by paying close attention. It considers body language, mirroring, and communication. Paco reminds us that no matter how well we read others, there will always be many inaccessible layers buried in the murky depths.

# 24

# "Blah Blah Hungry, Zeke?"
## *Sort through the fluff to get the main message*

oleridge's *Rime of the Ancient Mariner* includes the line, "Water water everywhere but not a drop to drink!"[68] The sailors are out of potable water onboard the vessel and look out at the expanse of the sea with its undrinkable salt water. A more modern version laments, "Data data everywhere but not a thought to think!"[69]

The technological revolution has brought us data on anything we can imagine. Now the challenge is what do we do with it all? What does it all mean? A leader faces the tough task of filtering through this onslaught of

[68] Coleridge 1798
[69] Shera n.d.

data and processing it to be able to use it as the basis for sound decisions. Studies point out that not only must leaders these days "gather, integrate, and interpret enormous amounts of information," they must then use what they've found to solve difficult problems and convince others to follow them using that same data.[70] It's not an enviable task.

One of Gary Larson's famous cartoons involves a dog owner fed up with his pooch's constant disruption of the trash bins. His finger pointing accusingly at the dog, he yells something like, "Ginger, I have had it with you getting into the garbage! You hear me Ginger? No more garbage! You stay out! Bad dog, Ginger!" The punch line is that all she hears of this is, "Ginger... *blah, blah, blah...*Ginger? *Blah, blah, blah, blah*, Ginger!"[71]

While the intent of the cartoon is to explain our frustration in communicating with our pets, I think it points out one of the advantages of being a dog. Dogs tend to sort through all of the extra fluff and get right to the important point of a message. In Ginger's world, the only relevant word is her name, so that's all she pulled out of the exchange. No matter what time of day, when I walk over to the toy basket and pick up the Frisbee, Paco knows we are going to the park. At that point no other messages matter—nothing that comes out of my mouth can distract him from the most important message. Uttering the words "hungry," "park," or "beach" have the same effect.

Zeke has also taught me how to search for the main message. Usually he snores his way through the whole night like a drugged sausage and needs to be persuaded to move in the morning. But every once in a while I'll be woken up at 3:00 a.m. by a wet nose in the eye. The first time this happened I ignored him—to my detriment. No less than fifteen minutes later I bolted upright, awakened by what smelled like an open sewer on a hot summer day. Zeke was telling me that he had eaten something foul and had to go out immediately. I misinterpreted him, thinking he was just bored and wouldn't let me sleep. That was a lesson I learned quickly. Poor Zeke was in dire straits

[70] Pierce and Newstrom 2008
[71] Larson n.d.

and because of my misinterpretation I had to leave a warm bed to clean up the contents of his intestines.

Leaders receive vast amounts of information from every channel—voice, e-mail, and print. The better ones learn to sort through this flood of data to quickly arrive at the relevant message, make a note of it, and move on. One of the first things taught in business school is creating concise messages for management.[72] The leader thinks, "Ok, I understand what you are saying, but how is this important? Why does it matter?" They cultivate an ability to extract only the pertinent message from all of the extra information delivered with it.

I worked with one very successful entrepreneur who had an uncanny ability to sort through all fluff and get directly to the point. He would sit quietly through a long presentation filled with graphs, data, and pretty pictures. His silence was intimidating as we knew he was listening to every word. After our dog and pony show, he'd zero in on the one part we missed. "That's all well and good," he'd challenge, "but your plan cannot work as long as our access to the RFID market remains as limited as it is presently. How do you intend to address that?" And in those few short words, he would have gotten to the heart of the matter.

This CEO's ability to drill down to the critical elements of each scenario was one of the keys to his tremendous success. No amount of smoke and mirrors could confuse him. Fancy talk and sizzle were pointless. By boiling down all the chatter to identify—and address—the core issues at hand he could work more efficiently. In a way there were more hours in his day than in ours.

While there is a time and a place for sociability and chitchat, the ability to turn this skill on and off as needed is a tremendous advantage. Successful leaders cut through distractions and everyday diversions and identify what

---

[72] This was the only test I failed upon entering business school. My liberal arts background had taught me to be loquacious and drawn out. Turns out managers don't like flowery language.

is most important. The best can decipher any topic of conversation—from social and political to financial and analytical—for the relevant point.

The skill extends beyond the workplace. For example, identifying the *real* reason your teenager is yelling at you helps to understand and better handle the situation.[73] Getting caught up in the words and emotions may only distract you from the real reason for the conflict. At worst it will draw you into a pointless argument. Or perhaps your spouse seems unreasonably upset that you left your milk glass out. Getting past the surface and to the heart of why there's so much emotion behind it can be a valuable skill. After all, it probably isn't just about the glass.

---

[73] In the case of teenagers, remember that their yelling is not rational 100 percent of the time.

# Lesson

Leaders have to process immense amounts of information and make decisions on faulty, contradictory, and incomplete information. While it isn't always possible to improve the quality of the data, it helps to learn how to cut through the fluff and try to identify the important elements of a conversation or presentation. What is the real message? What are the most critical elements? The easier you can "boil down" all of the incoming messages to discern the relevant parts, the faster you can make high-quality decisions. As you improve your ability to quickly address the real issues at hand, the quality and productivity of your communications should increase. Don't forget that a leader also serves as a filter of information to the rest of the organization, so once you identify the core issues, you can more effectively communicate them to others and direct them toward meaningful solutions.

# 25

## Paco See, Paco Do

*Matching your actions, tone, and mood to connect with others*

Dogs are very empathetic to their owners' moods. When my wife is upset, both Paco and Zeke make every attempt to console her. It may only be caused by a sad movie, but they come right up and match her mood in an attempt to make her feel better. This "mirroring" usually consists of sitting with her quietly and leaning on her. They share in her sorrow, even though they don't know where it came from.

Mirroring occurs when one person mimics the behavior or mannerisms of another. It may be intentional or unconscious. It may happen automatically. Maybe you are having coffee with someone, and when they lean forward, you do too. Or they raise their eyebrows to convey surprise in a story, and you lift yours too. At some level our body language shows that we are synched up with the other person, that we are sharing their emotional state of mind as it changes.

Your efforts to mirror your colleagues can also be consciously nurtured to make you a more effective leader. Your body language is constantly communicating whether you are speaking or not.[74] If you are aware of it, you can ensure that your gestures and your voice are saying the same thing. You can also send nonverbal messages to connect more deeply with others. Mirroring is one very effective way to do this.

Mirroring can also help you develop power as a leader. Leadership researchers identified five sources through which power can be acquired in social situations.[75] Called the bases of social power, they are:

1. **Reward power**: Based on one's ability to control rewards received by another

2. **Coercive power**: Based on one's ability to control punishments of another

3. **Legitimate power**: Based on one's perception that another has a legitimate right to power over them, for instance through their position (such as a policeman, a parent, or a boss)

4. **Referent power**: Based on one person's identification with another

5. **Expert power**: Based on the perception that one has special knowledge or experience in a certain area

Referent power stems from one person's identification with another person. The more I perceive you are like me, the more power I give you over me. Politicians use this all the time. When people described George W. Bush as

---

[74] See next chapter
[75] French Jr. and Raven 1959

"someone I'd like to grab a beer with," they were giving him referent power. In every primary, when candidates step up to the podium and tell you how much they are just like you, sharing your fears, hopes, and dreams, they are looking to increase their referent power and cash it in at the polls. Mirroring is a simple way to increase your own referent power.

The dogs mirror a wide range of emotions. When I'm excited, they're excited, even if they don't know why.[76] When I'm feeling down, they mope around. And when I'm inquisitive, they are too. Every time I try to figure out what toy is stuck under the couch, I get down on my hands and knees to peer under it. Zeke rushes up and head-butts me out of the way. *Oh boy! What are we looking at?* It's like a magician's hat—they never know what'll come out next. *Is it a squirrel? A bone! A steak!* It drives them bonkers. Whatever dusty object I retrieve is their favorite thing in the world for the next five minutes.

This behavior helps establish a bond between us. It's especially effective since we have limited language communication ability, so mirroring lets us know we're on the same page. Sometimes the extent of their mirroring is astonishing. For example, if I lie on the bed to read and happen to sigh, I usually hear another little sigh echo mine a few seconds later. It comes from Paco, stretched out on his bed in the corner, looking at me and wagging his tail. He's even participating in my relaxation!

There are two reasons why it's tricky to improve mirroring behavior. First, once you notice it, you see it everywhere and it drives you crazy. When you sit next to someone who leans back and crosses his arms you'll notice you have the urge to do the same. Then the thoughts come in: *Should I? Do I really want to, or am I just unconsciously mirroring? Will he notice? Has he studied body language? If so, what message am I sending?* It can make you awfully self-conscious at first, but this eventually fades as you get more comfortable with it.

---

[76] They usually don't.

The second reason it's tricky is that things can get awkward quickly if you are too obviously mirroring someone in an attempt to connect with them. It may appear forced. This, of course, reduces the connection between the two of you as the other person wonders why you scratch your nose every time they do, and why you sip your drink exactly as they sip. The key is subtlety—don't mirror everything.

It's no different in e-mail etiquette. When responding to an e-mail, notice how the sender signed off. If he wrote a formal "Sincerely, Trevor," then you probably want to respond in a similar way. If he just ended with his name, then match that. You want to meet them where they are, and little efforts like this make a big difference. Consider your position and theirs in the organizational chart. It's good to be a little more formal responding to an e-mail from someone higher up in the organization than you. Just because the owner of the company writes in all lower case letters and doesn't use punctuation doesn't mean you should too.

Part of my MBA education included a "business manners" formal lunch where we were taught the right way to dine. It was the closest I ever got to a finishing school experience. Some of the advice was bordering on hilarious. For example, it's apparently rude to bite directly from a buttered piece of bread. The correct form is to tear off a portion about the size of your thumb, butter it, and then put the whole morsel into your mouth. In between these mysterious gems of advice, we learned how to mirror. When your lunch guest finishes eating his or her food, you must stop eating as well, no matter how hungry you are or how much food is left on your plate. The idea is that you are signaling to your associate that you are in synch. *I see you've put your fork down. I too am done with my meal! Aren't we just two peas in a pod? Now let's close that deal...*I have to say I never used this particular piece of advice, because any possible benefit I'd gain from mirroring would be outweighed by my hunger-induced sour mood.

Previously we discussed self-monitoring, the ability to observe and manage one's own mood and presentation to others based on reading social cues. Mirroring is another form of self-monitoring. By better monitoring the needs and desires of others, you can more effectively meet those needs and satisfy those desires, which increases the chance you'll emerge as a leader (if you aren't one already) or be seen as an effective one (if you are).[77]

[77] Pierce and Newstrom 2008

# Lesson

Be aware of mirroring. Use it gently and subtly to connect with others. Handled appropriately, mirroring can show others that you share similarities, which can be beneficial both personally and professionally. Whether they know it or not, most people read body language very well and may judge you based just as much on what you do as what you say. One of the five bases of social power is referent power, defined as one's identification with another. The more others identify with you, the greater your referent power. Mirroring and other self-monitoring behaviors increase this social power.

# 26

🦴

# Getting Past "Woof"
*Nonverbal communication is still communication*

The best leaders are undoubtedly great communicators. But that communication extends beyond the spoken word. Leaders can embody their messages completely through action.[78] In this case a leader makes sure everything a follower might see (appearance, actions, gestures, attitudes) is in alignment, to ensure that nothing that is *seen* sends a different message than what is *said.* They make sure that they "walk the walk" in addition to just "talking the talk."

Dogs are masters at nonverbal communication. They are limited to only a small range of vocal options and must use body language to get their message across. We often forget that our bodies are constantly sending messages,

---

[78] Gardner 1995

with every move and action, whether we intend to or not. These signals come through loud and clear to our friends, family, and coworkers, so we might as well know what they are communicating. Some even claim that over half of the entire message that we communicate to another in person is in the form of nonverbal communication.[79]

A few years ago I picked up a book on body language[80] and read it cover to cover. In it, the authors outline all of the many ways our bodies can betray our true intentions and feelings. Everyone is aware of the crossed arms stance and how it transmits an unwillingness to be open to new ideas (at least in Western cultures). Imagine that you're in a meeting and listening to people critique your latest proposal. You may catch yourself leaning back in your chair with crossed arms and, in an effort to appear more open to suggestion, purposely uncross them. This may not be sufficient to convince everyone you are comfortable. If you shift your feet, point them toward the door, or simply keep your hands in front of you, palms down on the table, the message sent is that you're nervous, closed off, and ready to flee.[81] Smiling and nodding won't help much if you don't also turn your palms up, hands unclenched, on the table. Only then will your body communicate that you're open to new ideas and ready to listen and collaborate.

In this same meeting imagine your shoulder muscles are sore and you lean back, crossing your arms behind your head for a change of position. Innocent? Maybe. But you're communicating to everyone who can see you that you consider yourself dominant. By exposing your vulnerable sides, your primal brain is signaling that it doesn't see any threat of attack. You're confident and secure. Or are you? Maybe you're trying to bluff and you're actually insecure. Using signals of dominance to mask insecurity is common—think of how many people yell louder as they start to lose an

---

[79] Mehrabian 1971

[80] Pease and Pease 2006

[81] Restless feet signal nervousness, the direction they point indicate where you'd like to go (in this case, out the nearest exit), and downturned palms tell everyone you've already made a decision and are unwilling to consider alternatives.

argument. In more than a few meetings I've seen the threatened party try to defend his bruised ego by positioning dominantly and making dismissive comments. I can almost hear them think, *Don't show fear. You're better than them.* Consider the implications of this behavior in a business meeting or even a family discussion around the dinner table. Deals have fallen through for lesser reasons.

If you want to show that you're listening and considering what another has to say there are several strategies to use. Turn your body toward the other person and look directly at them. If you're sitting, clasp and hold your hands in front of you while resting your elbows on the table. If you put your two index fingers up (think of the children's game "here's the church, here's the steeple...") against your lips then it will send the message even more strongly that you are really considering and thinking about what the other is saying. Another way to convey this is to hold your chin with one hand while facing and looking at the person speaking. A little nodding and some up-and-down movement of the eyebrows goes a long way as well. Now, please note that I advocate *actually listening* to the person as well. These suggestions aren't meant to allow you to appear to be interested when you actually aren't. But as long as you are devoting full attention to someone, you might as well back it up with body language.

I have often accompanied my clients to meetings with important decision makers from other organizations. Even though I'm introduced at the beginning of the meeting as the consultant, and not senior management or an owner of the company, the VIP usually ends up talking directly to me after only a few minutes, only glancing at my client (often the president) periodically. This is because I intentionally communicated through body language that I was listening and interested in what they had to say, while the person I came with didn't. It can make a significant difference.

My dogs communicate clearly using the subtlest of body language. When I come home after having left the dogs alone for a while and Paco won't come within ten feet of me, I know that he has to go to the bathroom really badly.[82] Some of the techniques they use are actually pretty ingenious. Paco comes over and licks the air to show me that he's thirsty and the water bowl is empty. He even thanks me after he eats with a quick lick to my hand on his way from the food bowl to the other room.

Improving your body language increases the quality of communication between you and your dog. It's easy to assume that only verbal communication works with dogs, but they interpret your body as much, if not more, than your words. The best commands are a combination of verbal and physical actions. Merely saying "sit" to Zeke isn't nearly as effective as combining it with an open upturned hand held over his head. Even though he knows what the word means, it's like he doesn't quite believe me until I signal him to sit as well.

Like most people, I had a base understanding of body language, but it wasn't until I observed the dogs that I realized that it's very rare that we aren't communicating nonverbally. We don't use body language to back up our words as much as we use our vocabulary to back up what our bodies are saying. Travelers in an unfamiliar city are often advised not stop in the middle of the street to open a map or peer around with a confused expression if they are lost. Instead they should walk briskly and purposefully, with their head up, to the next store or convenient indoor location. Once inside, then they can open a map. Even though they may be lost and confused, it's important that they not *appear* to be. Even the pace of your walk and the direction of your gaze as you walk down the street sends signals. And it's best not to look vulnerable. Just ask any girl who has walked alone after nightfall in an urban setting. Even the friendliest women learn to put on a tough face when walking alone through the city at night, signaling to others that they can take care of themselves, *thank you very much.*

Leaders use body language to their advantage. Whether they have a natural talent or study and practice it, they know that communication is a full body, full-time exercise. An effective leader can transmit confidence and

---

[82] I learned this by trial and error, unfortunately.

support to his team by the way he carries himself. He can encourage openness and creativity by showing that he's truly listening and engaged in new ideas. The manager who implores his employees to come to him with ideas, and then sits, arms crossed, looking at the floor when they do does not get too far.

When's the last time you experienced someone's words not matching up to their body language? Was it the spouse who insists, "I'm *fine,*" while frostily looking out the window, back turned to you? Maybe it was the fast food employee who says with a scowl, "It's a great day at Burger World. Would you like to try a triple bacon fish stack? It's delicious." How about the last time you did it? Did anyone believe what you were saying?

Many times the same verbal response by two different people may mean two completely different things. Paco is very vocal, so when I pat him he may grumble and make low growling noises. Because I can read the rest of his body—wagging tail, playful pawing, indirect eye contact—I can tell that this is just his way of conveying affection and playfulness. There's no reason for concern. But the same low grumbling or growling from Zeke means the exact opposite. He's annoyed and wants to be left alone, usually to eat. His head and ears are down; his tail is still. It would be unwise to stick a hand in his face. Without knowing how to read the rest of the situation and body language, the two identical vocal responses may be confused.

This is especially true across cultures. A client of strong Italian descent once told me, "If I'm not yelling at you it means I don't love you. Only worry when I'm quiet." In contrast, John Alexander, an author on Swedish business practices, says that if a Swede is very upset she may say quietly, "Now you have me upset."[83] This means that something is *seriously wrong.* Merely reading body language isn't enough. You need to know the cultural context to truly understand the message being sent. Otherwise it would be awfully confusing to go from having an Italian boss to a Swedish one.

---

[83] Alexander 2008

# Lesson

Effective leaders know how to use and interpret body language to communicate more effectively with others. Ensure that what your mouth says and what your body says are in alignment. You will increase the power and effectiveness of your efforts, because your followers will be watching you closely and looking for inconsistencies. Aligning the two will save valuable time by avoiding misunderstandings. Learning how to read subtle body language in others is also a tremendous asset, as you can get the "real" message of how they feel, despite what they say. As much as half of a message delivered in person is nonverbal, so learning how to both use and read body language can increase effective communication tremendously. Consider cultural factors as well to best interpret and understand the intent, because one culture's body language may be completely different from another's.

# 27

# Babbling to Babies and Dogs
### *Conversation is an art*

Otherwise serious and sane adults turn in to babbling fools around babies. Filling the air with silly sounds and gestures, they don't expect any coherent response. Maybe just a giggle or smile. The babies are, for the most part, speechless companions, allowing the grown-up to be completely wacky. Imagine how hard it would be to remain goofy if the infant gave you a tired look and said, "Can you please try to be a little more serious?"

We can also speak gibberish to our animals with the comfort of knowing they won't judge us. I know I do. I call them by silly nicknames and ask them questions I know they can't answer: *Are you hungry Dingo? Are you a hungry*

*Dingo? Time to eat? Time for foodums? Let's get you some tasty treats!* Any outside observer would see that Paco leaves this exchange with his dignity intact, and I end up looking the fool. Why do we act this way around partners—pets, infants—whom we know can't respond? Does their silence encourage our behavior? Communication is a complex phenomenon, one that requires a bit of strategy to approach the right way.

Some time ago I had a client who loved to tell everyone what he thought. Meetings were littered with interruptions, longwinded stories, and opinions. I would accompany him to appointments with clients and business partners and watch as he bulldozed the conversation. Each interaction was a battle to be won. Despite this, he valued honest feedback and was humble enough to know he had room to improve. No sooner were we out of earshot and he'd ask, "Well, how'd I do?" Rarely had I encountered someone who was so assertive yet so open to criticism.

In one particularly aggressive meeting, the other party had given up on trying to compete for airtime. They gave up and fell silent for the last thirty minutes. He hadn't noticed. When we were in the car on the way back to the office I asked him why we set up the meeting at all.

"What did we go in to that meeting to accomplish?"

He responded, "We wanted to see whether they would be good partners for the Mateo project."

"So are they?"

"I think so, but I have my doubts."

"What did you learn about them that you didn't know before?"

"Well, they..." He was silent for a moment. "I guess I didn't learn much."

"Why not?"

He thought about it. "Well, they didn't say a whole lot, did they?"

"They tried to. Do they know more about you now?"

"I guess."

"Why?"

"Because I was doing most of the talking."

"Right. You took the time to tell them what you expected of them, who you are, and what the company stands for, but you didn't give them a chance to talk. You didn't come away with any new information."

"I guess I didn't."

"Considering that information is a form of power, who came out of the meeting with the upper hand?"

"They did. They know everything about me, but I don't know anything new about them."

"So did you accomplish your goal for the meeting? Do you find out if they might be good partners for the project?"

"No."

We discussed how every time he commandeered the conversation he was actually putting himself in a bad position. If he had held back a bit and let them talk more, they may have divulged valuable information. Silence creates a vacuum that everyone wants to fill. Don't always be the first to jump in to fill it.

Conversation is like a dance—it's a give and take. You and your partner move in unison, each bringing energy but moving smoothly together toward a common end. If one of you is *pushing, pushing, pushing,* the other one is falling over. It's awkward. If you dance with style, then you can slowly glide across the floor to where you want to be. If you tackle and drag your partner to where you want him to be, then you accomplish nothing. In the best case, you look like a fool. In the worst case they'll distance themselves from you and resent you. If you *dance* them there, then there's a greater chance they'll like where you've led them, because they'll have participated in and enjoyed the entire process.

Alternately conversation can be viewed as a tennis game. It's a volley. You send your ball over—*whack*—and then you wait for the return. The other party matches where the ball lands and hits it back—*whack*—to your side. You run to where the ball is now and hit it back—*whack*—to them. This makes for an interesting conversation and a fruitful one. Conversations like this go somewhere and accomplish something. As long as each party watches where the ball (the topic of the conversation) lands, they can take it and send it back in the direction they want. By communicating in this tennis match style you learn more about who you're dealing with. They learn about you as well, and together you move forward. If you're the only one talking, then you're like a tennis pitching machine set on high speed. You keep on sending over missives—*whump, whump, whump, whump*—and they have no chance to return them. They may try for a few minutes, but it won't last long. Eventually they'll drop their racket and walk away.

As an exercise in becoming a better communicator, try being very quiet around someone to really learn who they are. At minimum, ask questions and listen. Whenever the conversation turns to you, gently turn it back to them. People love to talk about themselves, and they hate silence in conversations. By taking a genuine interest in someone, consciously keeping the conversation focused on them, you can find out all kinds of interesting things about them.

I've been told that the best way to make a good first impression is by letting someone talk about themselves. After all, that's their favorite subject. If you can keep the conversation focused on what they like, think, and feel, then they leave thinking you're just about the best person in the world—never mind the fact that they don't know anything about you. They're on a high from being the center of attention, and that's what they remember. Speaking about themselves made them *feel* good, and everyone likes something that makes them happy.

My dominant client started to put this perspective into practice. He transitioned to seeing meetings as a volley. He made sure that once his point was made he paused to let the other party return the conversation. Meetings became more productive, and people saw him as more cooperative and pleasant business partner. He got more by doing less. Years later he still gushes about how well this technique works, and how much less effort he has to put into his meetings.

# Lesson

Consider your communication style. Are you commandeering the conversation? Do you speak more than half of the time? Ironically, getting your point across may be easier if you speak less. The more words you use, the more watered down your points become. As the adage states: "Be brilliant, be brief, and be gone." By approaching communication as a dance or a tennis match, a back and forth that is more style than brute force, you will come away with a better understanding of your conversation partner and better results for each side.

# 28

Whimpering in Your Blanket

*Recognizing the complexity in others*

Paco was separated too soon from his mother. We're not sure if he was the one who left first, or if he just followed his brother, but in any case he needed a little more time with mom to fully develop. We deal with the consequences—increased separation anxiety and whole lot of squeaking—daily. In order to truly understand his broken maternal relationship, all you have to do is watch him interact with his blanket.

Usually this is a nighttime activity. After dinner when we all settle in for a movie Paco disappears for a moment, only to parade back in with his ratty fleece. He plops on the floor, bunches it up between his paws, and licks and nurses a fold of the blanket. After a few minutes of kneading it with rapt self-absorption, he becomes completely motionless with his nose buried out of view and eyes closed. He lets out a deep and heavy sigh, now completely lost to the outside world, and begins a muffled whimper. It's heartbreaking. He's having a quiet cry as he revisits the few early memories he has of his mother. *Oh, those were the good old days… Mommy, you used to protect and feed us…We were so warm and safe…I miss you so much.*

Then the strangest thing happens. Unprovoked, he'll snap and start to growl at the blanket, loudly ripping it into long shreds and violently tossing them aside. *How dare you leave me! What an evil mother! I hate you!* His claws trap one end of it on the floor, and he tears into the damp blanket, rearing his head back with dramatic strength. The fit subsides, and it's back to whimpering into it, almost as if he was apologizing to it for his outburst. Back and forth he goes, from aggression to remorse. Eventually he'll lift his head, come back into reality, and leave the damp and degraded blanket in a heap behind him.

This dog clearly has some issues. Assuming that his blankie is indeed a stand-in mommy figure, they revolve around a swirl of sorrow, abandonment, and blame for puppyhood traumas. Short of finding a canine psychiatrist, we try to just let him work through what he has to. Truth be told, he comes out of his self-guided therapy sessions in a decent mood.

Who knows what's really going on in that grapefruit-sized skull? I'm not one to judge. Most of us are pretty complex, and there's no easy way to read others. Everyone is unique and multifaceted, even those who don't appear that way. In fact, the people who appear the most one-dimensional usually turn out to be the most complex. I worked with a guy a few years back who could only be described as terminally happy. We were in an office setting, and no amount of beige décor or mind-numbing routine fazed him. Every day was Christmas. New employees would all go through the same stages of dealing with him:

1. **Amusement**: *This guy is wacky—is he for real?*

2. **Annoyance**: *Can't he give it a rest?*

3. **Acceptance**: *That's just him, I guess*

4. **Endearment**: *That's our Harry!* and finally,

5. **Concern**: *Is this guy going to go postal one day? Should I be plotting my escape route?*

Many leadership texts go out of the way to remind us how everyone's different, then go on to offer universal advice and conclusions. No matter how many tips, tricks, and techniques you pick up on how to lead and read others, they will only be so useful. Many times there is so much variation in individuals that you have to go back the drawing board and try again, cobbling together pieces from this theory and that study.

Situational Leadership Theory states that the efficacy of a leader depends on the interplay of three factors:

1. The characteristics of the leader herself (traits, behavior, training, etc)

2. The situation (influence from the external environment), and

3. The characteristics of the followers.

This third factor is as difficult and murky as any one person can be. "Followers" are not one homogeneous bunch but an aggregate of complex individuals. Any leader hoping to create positive change needs to take this complexity into account.

# Lesson

It is great to learn generalities about leadership, but there are no simple answers. Every situation is unique and every person complex. Any simple answer or approach will likely leave out an important piece. Think of these theories as tools in a box. The more you have, the better prepared you are to tackle the challenge before you. Know that each situation will require a different combination of approaches. Take your time (when you can) and become better acquainted with those around you. You'll get a feel for them, and your intuition will fill in where instruction fails.

# IV

# Leading Others

Over the years the concept of leadership has evolved from focusing on the traits inherent in observable leaders[84] to a conception of leadership as a desirable situation that arises from the interaction between two or more people:

> ...leadership is not a matter of passive status, or of the mere possession of some combination of traits. It appears rather to be a working relationship among members of a group, in which the leader acquires status through active participation and demonstration of his capacity for carrying cooperative tasks through to completion.[85]

This section addresses ways that we can be most effective working with—and through—others. We'll look at the importance of choosing the right emotion-provoking words, of thinking strategically, and of reading emotions

---

[84] The "Great Man" theory, presumably called so because history seemed to forget that not all effective leaders were men, or even all that great.

[85] Stogdill 1948

in others. In addition, we will examine leadership distance, where your effectiveness depends on exactly how far ahead—or even behind—you are. The dogs teach us how to influence our bosses and remind us that clarity and consistency are important in communication.

We'll also look at why answers without questions are meaningless, and how Zeke knows exactly when he can jump on the couch and break the rules without consequences (and no—it isn't when we're not there!).

# 29

&—3

# Not Always the Top Dog
## *When to lead and when to follow*

When we take Paco and Zeke out for our morning walk, we have come to expect the same thing every day. Paco pulls ahead in his enthusiasm to get wherever we are going, while Zeke drags behind in his quest to sniff every discoloration on the sidewalk. In the unlucky event that just one of us takes both dogs for a walk at the same time, the result is usually that we end up in a pretzel position. In the worst cases it can feel like the old medieval torture technique of being drawn apart by horses, each limb pulled by a different beast in a different direction.

Every once in a while the dogs will change their behavior. Paco languishes behind to keep a better eye out for scraps of food in the street, and

Zeke pulls forward like an ox. These times, while infrequent, remind me that there are times to lead, and there are times to follow.

Often in our quest to improve ourselves, we forget that we don't need to be leaders in everything. We also don't need to lead all the time. We may have expertise in certain arenas and enjoy exhibiting our knowledge and capabilities. If we're not careful, this enthusiasm can overflow and result in a misguided sense of importance in other areas. In these times we may overstep our bounds, especially when there is another in the room who *is* an expert and a leader on that topic. The same confidence and authority that one can legitimately claim in his field of expertise, say surgery, may not translate into authority in another related field like hospital administration.

There's a well-known anecdote about Einstein's selective memory. At one point, an acquaintance asked for his phone number. Einstein responded that he did not know it. "How is it that you don't know something so simple?" the man responded in disbelief. "Well," Einstein replied, "why bother storing that information in my head when I can just look it up?"

In much the same way, we have to choose what we would like to lead and be experts in. Where we aren't competing, we have to be gracious and willing to pass the floor to another when the situation demands it. Let's go back to the surgeon example. Surgeons tend to think very highly of themselves. This confidence, I would argue, can actually help to make them a better doctor and may have served them well over the years. Let's say that a general surgeon became chief and took on the role of representing her department. In the monthly meetings, topics from all of the other departments may be discussed, including billing, radiology, finance, and operations. This chief surgeon would do well to recognize the bounds of her expertise and defer to the chief financial officer for financial matters.

This isn't to say that she shouldn't contribute, because collaboration and group input is one of the reasons for having such meetings. She should just know that in other disciplines—such as financial or operational settings—she may not be suited to lead the discussion. In fact, arrogance in such a situation where she may claim to know what's best for operations may weaken her appearance as a leader in her own field. Her peers might observe her making obvious errors of judgment and question her capabilities in her own role.

This extends past the workday as well. Nurses who accept the chief as a leader in the operating room may resist if she tries to command the table at the local bar on Friday afternoon. Paradoxically, if she's humble after work and actively supports a floor nurse as the "leader" of the evening's events, she'll gain more acceptance in everyone's eyes. They'll be more likely to defer to her workplace authority if she lets go when it no longer applies.

Sometimes the way to lead is actually to follow. In college, my friend Irene and I headed up a student organization. As with most collegiate groups, this one was composed of a motivated and dedicated base of individuals who believed in the group and its mission. With so many capable and strong-minded members, the group didn't need a commanding leader. It needed a president and vice president who coordinated the efforts of the members to create direction and planning. We merely facilitated the energy of the group, clearing obstacles and clarifying goals. The more soft-spoken and hands-off we were, the better. We learned to step back and follow the collective wisdom of our members. We were still there just in case we were needed, but we recognized that in order to develop this group and achieve its goals, we needed to lead 20 percent of the time, and follow our members the other 80 percent.

I've known many couples who have split up the "domains" of the household. She gets to lead the initiatives inside the house, and he gets full reign outside. Again, this doesn't mean that the other doesn't have a say. Rather they agree on who is the leader or follower in different situations. If it's time to change the garden beds along the side of the house, he gets to lead that initiative. But if the dining room needs to be painted, she leads the quest for the right color paint. They're both content with their roles and understanding of when it's appropriate for each to lead or follow.

# Lesson

Leadership, ironically, isn't all about being out in front. There are times to lead and times to follow. Know your strengths and your capabilities, but be aware of when it serves everyone better (including yourself) to graciously adopt the role of a follower to achieve desired goals—both yours and those of the whole group.

# 30

# How Old Is He...She?
## *Gender and leadership ability*

D o men make better leaders? Or do women? Who can lead a PTA meeting more effectively? What about a Fortune 100 company? Or an army? Does it matter?

Researchers have taken a few stabs at this question and have found that the answers aren't so clear cut. Previous studies seemed to indicate men were more likely to be leaders, but two researchers found that the opposite was true in their study: women were slightly more likely to emerge as leaders.[86] But their other finding was just as interesting. What matters more than biological sex (whether one is physically a man or a woman) is gender role (how you

---

[86] Kent and Moss 1994

act, how you rate on a scale of ultra-masculine to ultra-feminine). They found that "individuals characterized by androgynous and/or masculine attributes were more likely to emerge as leaders than those with feminine attributes."

So it seems that how masculine or feminine you *act* is the determining factor of how likely you are to become a leader. What about once you *are* a leader? Are there differences in performance? Another meta-study found that "male and female and female leaders are equally effective" but they "are not equally effective *in every situation*."[87] Women tended to perform better as leaders in democratic and participative environments, while men tended to excel in a more hierarchical, bureaucratic workplace. The authors note that both feminists and organizational consultants have been calling for more democratic and participative organizational structures, which, on casual observation, appears to be the direction companies are heading. This would indicate that women will be more and more effective as leaders as time goes on, and this style becomes the norm.

All of this research asks us to confront our own stereotypes about gender and leadership ability. It occurred to me that even with our pets we have these preconceived notions. When we address them head on, they seem ridiculous. Specifically, dogs are associated with masculinity and cats with femininity. On the face of it, there seems no reason that this should be the case. At the park I notice that people will more likely assume a dog is male, asking, "How old is he?" before being corrected otherwise by female dog owners.

Before Zeke, I had another rescue dog named Lucy. The first time I brought her up to Cape Cod for the summer my brother commented, "It's so funny to think of owning a female dog. All dogs are male in my head for some reason." We had grown up around only male dogs, so this may have contributed to the association, but it raises the question of why this conception is so common. Is a male cat any less feline? Is a female dog any

---

[87] Eagley and Johnson 1990, emphasis added

less of a canine? Do we have the same association with leaders as by default being men, with the high profile women (Hillary Clinton, Aung San Suu Kyi, Carly Fiorina, and the like) merely being the exceptions that prove the rule?[88]

---

[88] Another question raised is the notion of an aggressive women being characterized as a "bitch." Is this derogatory label placed on women who veer too far to the masculine side, therefore falling into the traditionally male canine category? What about when we call someone "catty?" Does this mean that they are embodying the worst of the female (feline) characteristics?

# Lesson

The role of gender in leadership is not completely clear. Studies show conflicting evidence on whether men or women are more likely to emerge as leaders. What seems to matter more is not the biological sex of a person, but how they act on a scale of masculine to feminine. Those who tended toward masculine and androgynous gender roles seem to be more likely to emerge as leaders. Male and female leaders perform at the same level overall, although in participative and democratic environments women tend to excel as leaders, while in bureaucratic and hierarchical organizations, men do. What's important is that you take a look at your own views on the matter and watch out for any preconceptions you may have that are unfounded. Men don't necessarily make better leaders, just as dogs aren't necessarily male (or masculine) and cats aren't necessarily female (or feminine).

# 31

Wanna Go to the Beach?

*Using emotion-provoking words*

The most effective leaders make a conscious effort to intersperse their language—both in formal speeches and in everyday communication—with powerful, impactful, and emotionally significant words. Steve Jobs was a master at using emotive words effectively. Carmine Gallo, a communication coach for brands such as Chase, Intel, and Clorox, created an entire book around Jobs' mastery.[89] He points out that simple, concrete, and emotionally charged words work best. Instead of merely describing a product as "better than the competitors," it's more effective to exclaim that it "*obliterates* the competition" and has "a *firestorm* of capabilities."

---

[89] Gallo 2010

# Get the Cookie, Paco!

Politicians keep their jobs by provoking emotional responses in their constituencies using only their words. Think back to the last powerful speech you heard a politician give. Maybe it was an inauguration speech or on the campaign trail, or something as simple as a sound bite given to a reporter. The words you heard were no accident. They were carefully chosen to produce desired emotional responses in you the listener (and voter). Robert Kennedy's speech to the City Club of Cleveland months before his assassination provides a poignant example of the importance of choosing impactful words. In the excerpt below I've highlighted the key words.

> This is a time of **shame** and **sorrow**. It is not a day for politics. I have saved this one opportunity, my only event of today, to speak briefly to you about the **mindless menace** of violence in America which again **stains** our land and every one of our lives.
>
> It is not the concern of any one race. The victims of the violence are black and white, rich and poor, young and old, famous and unknown. They are, most important of all, human beings whom other human beings **loved** and **needed**. No one—no matter where he lives or what he does—can be certain who will suffer from some **senseless** act of **bloodshed**. And yet it goes on and on and on in this country of ours.
>
> Why? What has violence ever accomplished? What has it ever created? No martyr's cause has ever been **stilled** by an **assassin's bullet**.
>
> No wrongs have ever been righted by riots and civil disorders. A sniper is only a **coward**, not a hero; and an uncontrolled, uncontrollable mob is only the voice of **madness**, not the voice of reason.[90]

---

[90] Kennedy 1968

The effects of emotion-provoking words are clear with the dogs. I grew up in Massachusetts near the ocean, and one of our dogs, Sunny, used to be set off like a bomb with the word "beach." It didn't matter if he was passed out in the corner on the floor, sleeping in the sun; if he heard someone utter "beach," he'd be up like a bolt and racing around the room. My brother and I used to tease him by stringing together long silly sentences of similar-sounding words. "Can you *teach* us *each* how to *reach* the *beach?*" The poor dog would be practically apoplectic with excitement.

Paco and Zeke are no different. Certain words provoke very strong emotional responses. The most impactful words are "walk," "park," "hungry," and our version of "Who's that?" If I whisper "Whoozat?" to either dog they jump up electrified and bark and run around the room to find whomever snuck in without them noticing.

There are plenty of business euphemisms that try to capitalize on softening language. "Let go" or "downsized" is better than "fired" or "laid off." Now some evil genius even came up with calling companywide layoffs "right-sizing." How can you feel bad when it's "right"? The effect of saying, "We'll weather this downturn and power through to prove to the world the champions we are" produces a much different effect than saying, "Times will be tough for a while but we'll survive and stay in business." Parents are naturals at this. They choose their words carefully to motivate their kids and soften tough news. After all, "Goldie's not with us anymore" is much kinder than, "Your fish died and I flushed it."

Slowly building emotionally powerful language and phrases into your everyday speech will make you a much more effective communicator and as a result, a better leader. Much of leadership is working through others to achieve results. This is best done through language to motivate and inspire.

# Lesson

Incorporating emotionally provoking language to your professional and everyday speech is a simple and effective way of increasing the power and weight of your words and the effectiveness of your communication skills, making you a more effective leader.

# 32

## What a Dog Wants
### *Thinking strategically*

S trategic leadership is a hot topic. Many of the chapters in this book are about strategy, in one way or another. Strategy involves understanding a range of objectives and balancing an approach with the realities of the external environment and any internal constraints. One common approach is the SWOT analysis. SWOT analyses set up a framework through which to evaluate a situation. By looking at the internal factors (your Strengths and Weaknesses) and the external (Opportunities and Threats you face), you can formulate a better strategy to deal with the present situation. Leaders who exhibit originality, creativity, nonconformity, and alertness—all central to strategic thinking and action—have been found to be more effective.[91]

---

[91] Judge, et al. 2002

I can often see these traits in the dogs. If Paco is still working on a bone that Zeke wants, Zeke employs a strategy that brings him success about 75 percent of the time. He knows that Paco is jealous for our attention, so he uses this character trait to lure Paco away from the bone. Zeke will come up to me, place his head in my lap, and give me a sad look until I pet him. If this doesn't work, he'll go grab a toy and bring it to me to play with. Once he has my attention, he'll glance back at Paco to make sure he's watching. Typically, it only takes two minutes of this before Paco runs abandons his bone and butts in to steal some of the attention. Zeke, waiting and watching for exactly the right moment, zips back to the bone and grabs it. Paco's lost the bone, and I feel a little used, but Zeke has gotten what he wants.

For Paco, it's a mixed blessing. Yes, he lost the bone, but he got attention from us. Since the bone is as much a way to get attention as it is an object to chew on, Paco in a sense may have won as well. But it is clear that Zeke is the initiator. He sees what he wants (the bone), reads the situation (Paco is a jealous dog for attention; I'm here to use as bait), and then executes his plan successfully.

In life there are a number of different ways that you can use strategy to achieve your goals. You can do as Zeke does and analyze your competition's likely behavior. You could also differentiate (see the chapter on creating your personal brand), setting yourself apart from others. You could align yourself strategically or aim to be the first mover, or imitate. Each strategy works differently depending on who uses it and in what situation. Paco fails miserably every time he uses the strategy of imitating Zeke because he is so obvious, but he excels at the "first mover advantage" strategy, as he's quicker than Zeke and uses Zeke's moments of hesitation to jump in and grab what he wants.

The better you are at thinking strategically, the further you advance in your objectives. Although there are times when you may be able to just power your way to your goal, as Zeke could have done to get the bone from Paco by using his strength, this tactic usually produces negative side effects as it is rough and clumsy. What you win by powering your way through may not be worth what you lose as a result of using that technique.

# Lesson

Know your goal, know your game, know your competition, use appropriate strategies. Rather than just going after the bone, which he could do easily with his size and dominant status, Zeke uses strategy to lure Paco away. Paco's strategy is first-mover advantage. He uses Zeke's suspicion of treats to jump in and eat Zeke's treat before Zeke can figure out whether he trusts it or not. Figure out which strategies work best for you and know the appropriate setting to apply them.

# 33

# Play-dar
*People like those who like them*

**M**y wife tells me that the Beach Boys song, "Good Vibrations," is actually about a dog's ability to pick up good or bad "vibes" from people and the importance of sending out good vibrations. I'm not sure if this is actually the origin of the song, but I agree with the intent. This is such a simple idea that we often miss it. People like those who like them. And, as we have seen in the previous chapter about body language, if you are only pretending to like someone to get on their good side, they can probably tell.

Anyone with a dog knows that dogs are experts at telling who is a "dog person" and who isn't. Those who come in the house and truly like dogs are immediately at the receiving end of affection, toys, and attention from our dogs. They are picked up on the "play-dar" and it's time for fun. But those who are unsure of dogs or just plain don't like them, are left alone or avoided after a quick sniff. No amount of "Nice, doggy" or stiff pats on the head can convince the dog that a guest likes dogs when they clearly do not.

People aren't all that different. Many times people make it clear that they do not like other people. Whether it is in social settings or work settings, many people actively send the message that they do not like another using body language, tone of voice, and even more obvious ways. There's nothing wrong with this in and of itself—you don't have to like everyone. As long as you don't mind if someone else knows that you don't like them, then you got your point across and that's that. The problem comes in when you pretend to like someone for whatever reason.

You may feel that you have to "make nice" with a superior, a client, a relative, or a friend of a friend. Maybe you are trying to avoid conflict, doing it for the sake of another, or maybe closing a deal depends on it. For whatever reason, you are much more likely to achieve your objective if you can find anything about that person to actually admire or respect. In most cases, any attempts to try to make nice to someone who you just can't stand will be obvious to them as fake.

Effective leaders are aware that others are more perceptive than most people give them credit for. So they look for that one aspect of a person that they show authentic respect to. For instance, you might find out that a miserable boss volunteers for the homeless twice a year. A petty or superficial coworker may have unconditional love for her adopted child. It may be something as simple as a common interest.

Research shows that the more similar the attitude of the leader to that of his followers, the higher the quality of relationship between the two.[92]

---

[92] Pierce and Newstrom 2008

Any married person reading this right now is probably slowly nodding in agreement.

In business school there was a classmate who just rubbed me the wrong way. I typically pride myself on relating well with most people, or if not, gracefully removing myself from contact with them. But this guy was in many of my classes and attended many of the same social functions as I did. I tried to find something about him that I liked, but I just couldn't. He seemed small-minded, mean-spirited, and antagonistic on every occasion I came in contact with him. We had to work together on group projects at times and I tried to be friendly, but it was clear that he could tell that I wasn't too fond of him.

One day a bunch of classmates got together at a local bar, and he was there. There were about fifteen of us, not enough so that the two of us could just ignore each other. I happened to come up to the bar for a drink while he was there too. We exchanged curt greetings, and then (maybe it was the drinks), we both acknowledged that there was this tension and distrust between us, and for no discernable reason.

Until then, I didn't know that he too felt this animosity between us. Abruptly, he said the most profound thing. He looked at me and said, "I think you and I are natural nemeses, in the true sense of the word. I always assume the worst about a person until he proves me wrong, and you always assume the best about a person until he proves you wrong. You generally like people, I generally don't. You generally trust people, and I generally don't." We eyed each other.

"True," I said. "Maybe I'm too optimistic and you are too pessimistic. Maybe there's something we need to learn from each other." He narrowed his eyes, stared hard at me, and said, "Yeah, I think you're right." And then I took my beer and we parted ways.

Even though we never really talked again, the tension was gone and when we passed each other in the halls we would exchange a quick hard glance that now conveyed respect between us. We still didn't really like each other, but we respected each other and that made all the difference.

Whether you call it energy, vibes, or just a feeling, people can tell when others truly like them or are just pretending, just as my dogs can. If you find yourself in a situation where you must be on good terms with someone you don't really like, take the effort to find something, *anything*, that you might respect about or have in common with them. Once you find it, it may be the basis for other commonalities or it may remain as the only thing that you find redeeming about them. In either case it will make all the difference in relations between you two. When you communicate with them or work with them, you will have that one aspect of them that allows you to be authentic in your efforts to like them. They will be able to tell.

Remember referent power from the chapter on mirroring? People not only like those who they identify with, but they actually accord them a form of power over them. It will help you to work with and through others when you find a commonality with them, but in doing so you are gaining a kind of social power that can be used to further influence them to attain common goals.

# Lesson

People are often better than you think at detecting superficial friendliness. There are times when you don't care, but there are other times when a good relationship with someone is very important for personal or professional reasons. Effective leaders look for an aspect of the other person that they can truly like, appreciate, or respect. It doesn't matter how small. That will be enough for you to authentically relate to the other person and improve your relationship, or at the very least effectively work with them. People like people who like them, so the more people you truly like, the more you will be liked and the more effective a leader you will be.

# 34

∽⊂∋

# Looking Guilty Together
*Taking one for the team*

Usually when we think of leaders we don't think of self-sacrifice. However, it has been shown that one of the best ways to increase employee effectiveness (as a leader) is to exhibit self-sacrificial behavior.[93] How could this be? Essentially organizations depend on the willingness of employees to sacrifice their own desires (for instance, to skip work and go to the beach on a nice day) in order to work on company goals (like sitting in a windowless office that same day to process data). When followers see that a leader is willing to make personal sacrifices for the attainment of the common goal, they interpret it as evidence that the goal is worthwhile and that they're all in it together. As a result they are more likely to put in

---
[93] De Cremer and van Knippenberg 2004

extra time and effort toward the goal. But if a leader skips out early to go to his son's football practice while the rest of the employees have to stay late for a deadline, that same leader is sending the message that he looks at the employees merely as labor. In response, the employees are less likely to work effectively toward a company goal.

This is similar to when Michaele and I leave the dogs alone to go out for a while. They can get frustrated when they aren't allowed to come with us, and sometimes when we return they find ways to exhibit their displeasure. They each have their own signature way of letting us know they're angry. When we lived in San Francisco, we used to talk about Zeke having an internal "timer." If we left him for what he determined what was too long, he would choose one pillow, either off the bed or the couch, and tear it to bottle-cap sized pieces, spread evenly over the whole room. Paco, on the other hand, is less destructive in general but may have a hand in the mayhem.

The first few times we came home and a box, a toy, a bag, or some other item was destroyed as a way of communicating their frustration with us, we were not sure who was to blame. After all, we didn't *see* Zeke destroy anything, even though it was a safe bet that he was the culprit. So we tended to say, "No, bad dog," to both of them in general. Paco probably wasn't part of it, but in any case he shared in the shame and admonishment because he knows he's part of the "team." We were hoping one culprit would look guiltier than the other, but they both acted equally regretful and pathetic.

Sometimes part of being a good leader is sharing in the mutual pain of your team, even if you are not the cause. For example, if you are leading your team and they fall short of their goal due to the obvious actions of one or two people on the team, there are two approaches to responding to outside criticism. The first would be to single out the "weak links"—the cause of the group failure—and hang them out to dry by putting all the blame on them. This may deflect the blame from the others in this particular instance, but it will tear apart the team by creating divisiveness and fear.

The other option would be to accept blame as the leader for the performance of the team in general and to turn the attention toward doing a better job next time. While everyone shares partially in the blame, with the majority falling on you as the leader, this can help to foster team cohesion and loyalty to you as the leader. The members will see that you are willing to stand up and protect them and as a result they may feel more willingness to work hard for you.

Some studies seem to indicate that rewarding and punishing individuals in a group can increase that individual's performance while creating dysfunctional effects on the group as a whole.[94] This is because when individuals know they will be singled out for effort, they start to focus more on their individual goals, and less on group goals. It becomes "every man for himself," and the collective goals get left in the dust.

Other research suggests that individuals are more attracted to groups when they receive rewards while in the presence of other team members. They also find those groups more cohesive.[95] This makes sense. If I were to be rewarded in front of my team, I would have good feelings about the team and may even feel more connected to them (and therefore rate the team as being cohesive). Another study finds that when leaders reward or punish groups based on their performance, those groups' productivity goes up.[96] The authors of the study suggest that this may happen because when leaders use rewards and punishment, they are communicating to the team whether their performance met expectations or not. Either way, the team has more clarification on expectations and adjusts their goal setting accordingly. Increased goal setting then leads to higher performance. If you're my boss, the better I know what your expectations are of me, the more specific and relevant my actions can be toward attaining those goals.

---

[94] Schelling 1971
[95] Pierce and Newstrom 2008
[96] Locke, Cartledge and Knerr 1970

# Lesson

As a leader, there are times when you have to take one for the team. Part of your role is looking past short-term unpleasantness to determine what is best for the whole team in the long run. Although it is difficult at the time, directing blame away from others and onto yourself will increase loyalty and commitment of others by showing them that no individual, not even the leader, is more important than the group as a whole. When you show that you subordinate your own personal goals to those of the team, you increase their motivation and commitment to putting their own effort toward company goals. If you do have to use rewards and punishments with your team, make them clearly contingent on the performance of the team. Doing so will clarify your expectations to them and should result in higher performance.

# 35

## When to Jump on the Couch
### *Reading and responding to the emotional element*

Ask anyone what they think the most basic element of an organization is. They will probably (and correctly) skip past functional units like sales and HR and tell you, "Why, it's the people, of course." Yes, but dig a little bit deeper. What is the most basic element of people? I don't mean water, or carbon, or anything like that. It's emotions.

Emotions are the basic building blocks of people's actions. Those accumulated actions, added up across all the employees, managers, and owners (even the temps!), give that organization a personality, a trajectory, and a performance level. They also define how we perceive the organization from the outside. Consider the following examples.

- If the customer service rep on the other end of the phone is in a terrible mood, what is going to happen to your impression of the company?

- The greed and competitiveness—as well as the lack of empathy and ethic—at Enron affected thousands.

- If you meet a barista who is genuinely happy (maybe he just went on a great date last night) and greets you with a heartfelt, "Good morning!" You may just walk out of that coffee shop with a bounce in your step.

Human emotions are at the core of everything. So why is this important? Bad leaders ignore emotion altogether and may actively implement strategies that disregard emotional consequences—for example, the little league coach who rules by fear and intimidation. Mediocre leaders are aware that emotions matter but have no idea how to handle them. The best leaders, however, acknowledge and respect employees as whole people, and in doing so create policies, interactions, and strategies that increase organizational performance.

Just as you can't correct someone's grammar in Japanese if you don't speak the language, a leader can't recognize what it means for an employee to be "whole" if they aren't whole themselves. This is why many leadership development programs focus on creating a more  rounded person. It starts at the top, with the leader, and once he or she becomes more rounded and complete, then it is possible to recognize this need in others. And once they do, the organization improves.

In leadership research, this emotional element appears in two significant ways. First, many scholars have identified "consideration" as one of the most important leader traits. The trait of consideration can be roughly described as "behavior indicative of friendship, mutual trust, respect, and warmth."[97] A meta-study completed in 1994 concludes that consideration has "important

---

[97] Bowers and Seashore 1966

main effects on numerous criteria that most would argue are fundamental indicators of effective leadership."[98] In other words, the more considerate you are, the greater the chances you will be an effective leader.

The other area where emotion arises in the research is emotional intelligence. It is defined as "the ability to perceive emotions, to access and generate emotions to assist thought, to understand emotions and emotional knowledge, and to regulate emotions reflectively to promote emotional and intellectual growth."[99] The idea is that the emotional world is at the basis of many human decision-making processes. The ability to communicate in this world and navigate it effectively makes one a more effective leader. Emotional intelligence has been shown to have a role in "leader emergence," when a team member emerges as the leader of a group.[100]

If you still aren't convinced that emotions make a big impact, consider the results of a study[101] from Rensselaer Polytechnic Institute's School of Management. Entrepreneurs were ranked in terms how expressive they were and how good they were at reading emotions. Those who scored in the top 10 percent (the "most expressive") earned on average $250,000 a year, while the bottom 10 percent (the "least expressive") earned on average $175,000 a year, a full *seventy-five thousand dollars less!* The ability to read emotions seems to be even more important. Those where in the top 10 percent (the "best at reading emotions") earned on average $225,000 a year, while the bottom 10 percent (the "worst at reading emotions") earned only $100,000 a year, *only 44 percent as much!* Makes you want to improve your ability to read emotions a bit, doesn't it?

Dogs are naturals at being able to tell when you need emotional support and encouragement. They read your body language, which is sometimes subtle and sometimes obvious, and respond with unconditional support.

---

[98] House and Podsakoff 1994
[99] Tapia 2001
[100] Wolff, Pescosolide and Druskat 2002
[101] Rensselaer Polytechnic Institute 2001

Sometimes all it takes is a sad movie, and Zeke picks up on Michaele's distress. He plods slowly and somberly, sits directly facing her, and buries his head in her lap. If this doesn't work, he jumps up on the couch (which he knows is not allowed) and licks her in the face to cheer her up. His concern for making her feel better is so strong that he's willing to risk being punished for breaking the rules just to be able to comfort her.

As a leader there are times for strategy and unemotional analysis. But there are also times for genuine compassion and concern for your team. Everybody has their times of personal difficulty when their mind is not on the task at hand. What they need is to see that even at the office, or otherwise in their professional life, they have support. There's no need to pry into why or to get too involved. A few simple words indicating that you realize that they are not in top form is sufficient. Show that you see them as more than just another employee to help build loyalty and dedication to the team.

# Lesson

Don't forget the emotional element in life. If you trace back any action far enough, you will find emotion at its core. The dogs are naturally astute at picking up our emotions. Since they don't speak our language, they have to use other methods for communicating with us. It's easy to assume that since you speak the same language as others in your office, you're communicating. This may not always be the case. In addition to paying attention to body language, learning to pick up on and appropriately respond to emotions in others should reap tremendous benefits. Not only should managing through others be easier, but they should see you as more effective in your role as well. Studies have shown that the more emotionally intelligent an individual is, the greater the chances they will be an effective leader. Research has also identified the extent to which a person is considerate to be an important indicator of how well they are able to lead (and how much money they can make).

# 36

Twenty Steps in Advance

*Leading at just the right distance*

Zeke is not the sharpest knife in the drawer. He's very cute and endearing, but he can really be dumb as a post sometimes. Case in point: he can get lost in our house. To be fair, many times when he's turned around, it's not because he doesn't know where *he* is, it's because he doesn't know where *I* am. Our staircase is in the center of the house and is split into two sections with a landing in between. You walk up, turn ninety degrees right on the landing, walk a few feet, turn ninety degrees again, and walk the rest of the way up. If I'm upstairs and I call Zeke, he has trouble triangulating where I am. Did my voice come from upstairs? Or from the other room? He'll run halfway up to the landing and wait. When I call him again he knows I'm upstairs, but now my voice is coming from the direction where, if he ran toward me, he would be *descending* the stairs. Now he's completely baffled. Should he run toward my voice and down to the first level, or away from my voice and up to the second level (where he now knows I am)? It's just *so confusing.* I have to literally walk down to the landing and guide him up, so that he can follow me in the right direction, and the stairs line up with the path to my voice. Like I said, he's not brilliant.

The same thing happens when we are out for a hike. The best places are off-leash areas where the dogs can run free without danger of traffic or unsuspecting pedestrians. Many of these locations are in the woods, composed of a network of small footpaths.

Taking Paco and Zeke on the trails is predictable. Paco zips back and forth, running a hundred feet ahead, then coming back and checking on us before running ahead again. He usually gets twice the walk we do. Zeke usually falls behind, engrossed in the smell of some patch of ground.[102]

For most of the walk, we don't have to worry about the dogs. They run off and play and then catch up with us again. Yet we have to take care when there's a fork in the path. Paco is usually attentive enough so that if he's ahead of us on the wrong fork he zips back and finds us. Zeke gets lost. Since he lags behind, he doesn't see which path we took. His solution is to panic, choose a direction, and just sprint.

We first observed this on the trails at Fort Funston in San Francisco. This park remains our all-time favorite place for dog walking. Stretching out on rolling cliffs and dunes over the Pacific Ocean, the paved paths are a magnet for dog owners. The dogs socialize while the people get a workout and a stunning view.

One afternoon we were hiking there with the dogs, and Zeke fell behind. We didn't notice for a few minutes, and when we did turn to look for him, we

---

[102] We've nicknamed him Ferdinand, after the bull in the children's book who'd rather sniff flowers than fight.

could barely see him around a bend. At that moment he looked up from the root he was sniffing and realized he had lost us. We saw the panic set in as he frantically scanned everyone around, not finding us among them. Within ten seconds he simply chose a direction (the wrong one) and took off at full speed. There he went, sprinting his muscular little body off into the distance, his head glancing at every person he passed.

Leaders need to be just far enough ahead of their followers to motivate them, inspire them, and show them the direction, but not so far that nobody can see them. This quote by Georg Brandes, an influential Danish literary critic, sums it up nicely: "The crowd will follow a leader who marches twenty steps in advance, but if he is a thousand steps in front of them, they do not see him and do not follow him."

When we were a hundred feet in front of Zeke, he was able to follow us. Once we got too far ahead of him, we lost him. When a leader is no longer in sight, some followers will behave as Zeke did—they will choose a direction and just run. Others will sit down and wait. In any case, the leader will no longer be a leader as there is no one following him.

In many cases, the "distance" between a leader and followers is not literal. It may be the distance between the mindset of the two. It may be a gap in vision. For instance, Steve Jobs may have lost some followers who did not grasp his vision of personal computing. Transformational leaders are aware that while they have to push the envelope they still need to communicate a future that followers can identify with and understand.

So how do leaders provide a path for followers to show them how to get from point A to point B? I have to meet Zeke halfway down the stairs to correctly guide him, and it's not too different for the leader of a (human) team. Leaders meet their followers halfway and provide them structure and direction. They initiate structure by putting organizational elements in place and clarifying vision and goals toward which everyone should strive. Initiating structure (along with consideration) has been found to be one of the most important elements of effective leadership.[103] It consists of organizing and communicating within an organization how work is supposed to flow and what tools, policies, and procedures are available to guide that workflow. In general, initiating structure means making clear to everyone how tasks are supposed to get done, providing a path of here to there. For instance, a company goal may be to increase gross revenue. OK, how? Make more sales calls? Make the same number but make them better? Attend more networking events? Put money into research and development of new products? New services? Who should they ask to clarify? When left without any intermediate direction and structure, employees have to guess for themselves how best to achieve this collective goal of increased gross revenue. When this happens, inefficiencies result. If a leader steps in and initiates structure, efforts can be aligned. The key is to lead at just the right distance—not so close as to be micromanaging but not so far as to be vague and unclear.

---

[103] Bowers and Seashore 1966

# Lesson

As a leader you must stay in tune with the needs and desires of followers. But you must not get too far ahead of them, or you will lose them. They need to be able to keep you in sight and see the path from where they are to where you are. If they can't see you or the path to get to you, they won't be able to follow you and will never reach the end goals. Leaders meet followers halfway by initiating structure and providing guidance in the organization to clarify how tasks are supposed to get done. Don't just tell people what you want done; give them the tools to perform and ensure they know how to use them.

# 37

# Who is Walking Whom?
*Influence works in any direction*

A good leader knows how to use influence. After all, if a leader is to get things done, they need to know how to direct and motivate others. A leader's use of influence "stems from his or her ability (or perceived ability) to exercise reward, coercive, referent, expert, and/or legitimate power."[104] As you may remember from the chapter "Paco See, Paco Do," these five types of power are referred to as the bases of social power. When you have (or are believed to have) any of these types of power, then you can use them to exert influence over others. But as we'll see, subordinates (and dogs) may be able to wield many of these bases of power over their superiors, thereby influencing upwards.

---

[104] Pierce and Newstrom 2008

# Get the Cookie, Paco!

Paco likes to carry his leash in his mouth, prancing ahead of us as we walk. Invariably, someone sees this and remarks, "Looks like *he's* walking *you!*" There's really no response for this, other than "Hehe, yep," or "Don't I know it!" My owner/pet relationship has also been questioned by my father. Upon observing me on "poop patrol" walking around the yard with a scoop and a plastic bag, he commented, "If aliens came down right now and saw this they'd think that Zeke owns you and not the other way around."

The traditional dog/master power structure is subject to confusion at times. It isn't as rigid as it appears. Using persuasion, either Zeke or Paco can motivate us away from the computer and out to play. We may be dominant over them, but they can still influence us upwards. Often it is assumed that one can only use influence from the top down. In other words, if you are a manager, you can exert influence over those who report to you, but not over those who are above you or are in positions equal to yours. But this is far from the case. Influence can be used from any position in an organization and in any direction. There are techniques that we can use to influence those above us in the power structure.

There are two sources of follower power: personal and positional.[105] Personal power stems from knowledge, expertise, effort, and persuasion. Positional power includes location, information, and access. Each of these has value to the leader and is held by the subordinate. The computer-whiz teenager has power over her boss who is still running Windows 95. A new employee who exhibits a high drive to learn can quickly gain influence in the eyes of his superiors. Even something as simple as where your desk is located can contribute to your power at work. The executive assistant to the president has tremendous power by being able to regulate access to his office. There's a reason that salespeople make friends with the kid sitting at the front desk. Think of the power of the information technology guy. He can see into everyone's e-mail accounts and browsing history, even the top level of the organization.

---

[105] Daft 2005

Much influencing upwards is based on being a resource to your superior. If you can make him look better, he will keep you close and be more receptive to your ideas. The employee who dedicates effort to improving their leader will rise up with him. As value is added, others will start to pay attention. With a record of success, an employee may even respectfully challenge authority. When I was single and taking Zeke out for walks, he attracted all kinds of attention from women. From a positional power perspective, his access to attractive women was better than mine, so he had a measure of power over me. He could break the ice better than anything I could do alone, so he was a resource for me. Of course, he never knew to wield this influence, but the point is that he could have.

A Greek friend of mine remarked that in her family, the father was the traditional head of the family.[106] But, she continued, her mother was the "neck" of the family, and could turn the head in any direction she wanted. Just because you aren't the head doesn't mean you can't help direct where it looks.

Research suggests that subordinate performance can even affect leader behavior.[107] The more poorly a subordinate (or group of subordinates) performs, the less consideration a leader tends to show toward them. We've seen this already when discussing in-groups and out-groups: when a leader gives a task to a follower and that task is not completed satisfactorily, the leader devalues that follower by placing them in the out-group. Not only does the leader show less consideration, they tend to impose more structure on the subordinate. The reasoning goes that poor performance may be due to lack of direction and structure in the organization. However, the opposite is true as well. Higher subordinate performance results in more consideration by the leader and a smaller chance he will impose structure (as there is no need).

---

[106] My wife tells me this same saying is in the movie, *My Big Fat Greek Wedding*. Maybe it's a common Greek idea?
[107] Greene 1975

# Lesson

You can influence from anywhere in an organization. To influence upwards, work on gaining knowledge that you can then turn into expertise through a history of successes. With a record of contributing to the organization and especially making your boss succeed, you begin to gain power. With it you can better influence the organization and ultimately become a resource for the leader. Think about where you sit at work. Are you in the flow of information? This could be virtual as well as physical. Position yourself centrally and network from there. As a subordinate, help your leader succeed by speaking openly and honestly. Let them know what you need to be a good follower, as good followers are the foundation of great leaders.

# 38

Dog's Dependence

*Accruing power*

Power is a defining element of the leadership process. This may seem obvious, but the reasons why are fascinating. Of course power allows a leader to impose his will upon others, and this can help achieve goals (at least in the short run, before everyone leaves at their first chance). But power also *allows a leader to define reality for others*. Think about that. We often think of reality as a solid and independent state outside of our perception. After all, when we close our eyes, reality is still out there, right? So how can it be open to definition by another person? A leader defines reality by interpreting events for others and weaving those interpretations into a narrative that serves as a basis for action. Once you understand this, you begin to see it everywhere.

Politicians are masters at trying to twist—I'm sorry, *interpret*—events for others and tie them together to serve their own needs. They take what the average person sees (let's say a rising unemployment rate), tell everyone what that event means, and how it ties into a greater story. Republicans would say unemployment is rising because we can't control immigration and undocumented workers are taking your jobs. Democrats say it is rising because there isn't enough money available from taxes to fund public job programs. Every day's news becomes a fight to make the salient events fit into the story. Those narratives then become a basis for action Republicans argue that we need to have tougher laws against immigration. If elected, they'll do that. Democrats would insist on raising taxes on the wealthy and put more money into stimulus packages. Elect a Democrat to get this done.

One study points out that not only do leaders try to interpret events and create reality for others, but in order for that leader to be successful a follower must *give up his or her own ability to interpret reality and accept the leader's version instead.* The authors state:

> We see the way the power relations embedded in a leadership role oblige others to take particular note of the sense-making activities emanating from that role. We have characterized this in terms of a dependency relation between leaders and led, in which the leader's sense-making activities assume priority over the sense making activities of others.[108]

So if you want to lead others, consider what events they are seeing and how those events support a story that will encourage them to behave in a certain way (but remember to be ethical!). If you must reduce overhead expenses, perhaps there are only two options: laying off 20 percent of the workforce or having everyone accept to work only four days a week so that no one has to lose their job. If you want to make the latter plan work, you might call an organization-wide meeting and explain that due to the economic downturn,

---

[108] Smircich and Morgan 1982

increasing competition from overseas competitors, and a shift in consumer tastes (all "events" that they can see for themselves), the reality is that the company needs to cut overhead costs by 20 percent to survive. Next, you might explain that this means that either one in five of them must be let go, or they all must go to four days a week of work for now. Ask them to look around and try to choose who they would lay off. Should it be the oldest and most expensive employees? The young ones who may be starting families? Again, they will know people in each category, and you will be interpreting these observations for them, and telling them that they may choose an option where no one has to be let go. Finally, you may seal the deal by telling them you too (and the rest of the executive staff) will share in the pain by taking a pay cut as well. With any luck, your speech will motivate them toward choosing the option that you felt from the beginning was best.

But interpreting reality for others isn't the only way to accrue power. Another way is to create circumstances where others are dependent on you. If they need what you have and can only get it from you, you've increased your power. This can be handled two ways—one is to convince others you have what they want (create need) and the other is to find a way to acquire or control what they actually already wanted.

Gaining power over the dogs is easy. Just by virtue of the fact that we feed them and control access to shelter gives us tremendous power. But aside from these basic needs, I can easily convince them that I hold the keys to other desirable outcomes. If I walk in with a plastic shopping bag and rustle my hand around in it while excitedly asking, "*What's this?*" they will climb all over each other to be the closest to the bag. Paco will literally push Zeke's head down and stand on his back. *Me first!* I've created the simplest form of power simply by persuading them that whatever it is that I have, they want. It is worth trampling your brother to get the mystery treat in the plastic bag.

How is power being used over you? Are others convincing you that they have what you want? Ask yourself if you really want what is being dangled in front of you, or if you just think you do. Try to break free and decide for yourself what it is you actually want. Power works both ways; you want to reduce how much others have over you while increasing your own power. Lowering others' power over you increases your own.

In the leadership literature a model has been developed that helps to explain how it is that certain people (and groups) obtain power and how they hold on to it. It's called the strategic-contingency model of power.[109] It states that power arises from when one person (or group of people such as a department) are best able to cope with a crisis and are therefore given the resources to deal with the crisis and move past it. When the resources are all moved to this party, they can use those resources to secure a long-term position of power. Let's take a look at an example.

Suppose there's a large company called Overseas Associates that deals in buying and selling natural gas products. In order to do so, they rely heavily on the use of contracts. Imagine there's a change in legislation and as a result much of the last six months of contracts may be invalid. This certainly qualifies as a crisis: without the contracts, the company can't get paid. The CEO looks to the department who could best handle this crisis—the legal department. Currently the legal department has two people. The head counsel recognizes that this is an opportunity to seize power. He meets with the CEO and tells him that the problem could be extremely bad and could cause ripple effects across all of their contracts—even the ones older than six months old—if customers find out that there's problem. They must act fast. He needs a budget of $1 million and needs to hire two more legal staff immediately. The CEO concedes. After all, it's a crisis and only the legal team knows how to solve it. After hiring the additional staff and securing the emergency budget, the head council quickly resolves the issue by creating and sending out to all current clients an innocuous-looking addendum to the contract. Crisis averted. But rather than telling the CEO right out that the problem is solved, he plays up the issue of the older clients (which may or may not really be a problem). The counsel tells the CEO that it will take nine months with

[109] Salancik and Pfeffer 2005

his new team to review all the old contracts to make sure they are secure, and in the meantime it would be a good idea if the CEO runs all of his company strategy past the counsel, just to be safe. Over the next months the counsel meets constantly with the CEO, sitting in on meetings and decisions. He uses the information he learns to keep the CEO worried about other potential problems, thus essentially securing his position as the second in command of the organization. In this way the head counsel, and by extension the legal department, used a crisis to first gain resources and influence and then secure a position of power for the long term.

Power, like a leader, is not inherently good or bad. How it is wielded and to what ends determines whether we consider it ethical or unethical. Power is potential.

# Lesson

There are several ways to accrue power. First, you can interpret events for others, and by doing so weave those events into a narrative that serves as a basis for action. In essence, you provide a version of reality that is so compelling to others that they choose your version over their own. Second, you can control resources that others need or desire. In times of crisis, the power lies in the hands of the person with the solution. If a group gets lost in the woods and only one person knows the way out, she is automatically the leader and the one with the most power. You can reduce the power others have over you by deciding for yourself what you desire, and why. There's nothing wrong with accruing power, but with it comes an ethical responsibility to use it the right way. Consider how badly a golden retriever wants a tennis ball, and what he'll do for it. In the end, it's just a ball. Are you letting others control your behavior in the same way?

# 39

# "Wait" Doesn't Mean "Stop"
## Communicating with clarity and consistency

My parents live on a hill overlooking a lake. When we take the dogs there for a walk, they go bolting down the winding path to the water. Since there is a small road between the bottom of the path and the beach, we have to watch out for traffic. As he sprints down, we tell Paco to "wait" so he won't just run in front of a car. Usually he's good about listening, but every so often I forget and use another word or phrase: *Paco, hold up! Paco, stop!* or *Paco, stay!* While these all mean the same thing to me in this situation, the only word that works for him is *wait*. His vocabulary is basic, and he doesn't really understand multiple words used for the same command. For years I told him "down" to get off the couch, not knowing that command meant *lie down where you are*. Michaele had already taught him the command "off" for those times he was on furniture—or people—and shouldn't be. Over time I've learned to be clear and consistent with him.

It's hard not to use many different phrases to ask the dogs to do the same thing. They understand one, but too many gets confusing. For Zeke it's the same thing. *Sit-stay* makes sense to him. Any variation is completely baffling: *Hold it. Stay there. Don't move. Be still. Not yet.* The way they learn is through consistent use of one term.

While we humans are a little better at nuances and multiple meanings from one word, it still helps to be clear and consistent with your language. The best leaders are great communicators. They choose the right message, consider the audience, and make sure that what they're asking for contributes to the desired outcome. Poor communicators leave others guessing as to what they actually mean. This leaves room for interpretation and possible misunderstanding. In many cases leaders are not questioned or asked for clarification, so when there is confusion it leads to mistakes. For this reason another priority of effective leaders is fostering a climate of open communication where it isn't taboo to say, "What do you mean exactly?"

Choosing the right communication channel is also important. While most interaction between dog and owner is verbal, the manager has many more options. E-mail, voice mail, phone calls, texts, Twitter, and face-to-face communication are just a few options. Posted notices and even rumor and word-of-mouth are also other ways to pass a message along. Consider the best medium, or channel, for your message. A quick reminder to a peer might be best done by text, but a quarterly performance review should be done in person. When the tone of voice is important, its best to avoid e-mail, as misunderstanding is common.

Even small punctuation can make a big difference. A colleague of mine sent out a report to upper management via e-mail. She then realized that she had to make one last change so she updated it and sent out another version to everyone, asking them to disregard the old one. The CEO opened up the old version and pointed out that it needed to be updated. She e-mailed back to him, "I resent it." He came down to her office in person and demanded to know why she was resentful of him pointing out an error in her report. He thought she needed an attitude adjustment. What she meant was "I re-sent it." It took a little explaining, but the damage was undone. She learned her lesson, though. Aside from watching her punctuation a little more closely, if she had picked up the phone and told him she re-sent it, he would not have misunderstood her.

Leaders use communication as a basis for all that they do. They inspire, motivate, and direct people through language, aligning them to common goals and values. Effective communication is critical to good leadership. Organizational culture is top-down, meaning that the strengths and weaknesses of the leader trickle down to affect all aspects of day-to-day operation. When communication is poor at the top, the results can be disastrous. Sometimes even the best communicators can make the worst leaders if they use their talent for unethical ends. History is strewn with great orators who could advance their unethical agenda by mesmerizing followers with great speeches.

Leadership scholars have identified several ways that a leader's great communicative ability could become a liability for an organization:[110]

- Exaggerated self-descriptions

- Exaggerated claims for the vision

- A technique of fulfilling stereotypes and images of uniqueness to manipulate audiences

- A habit of gaining commitment by restricting negative information and maximizing positive information

---

[110] This entire list is from Conger 1990

- Creation of an illusion of control through affirming information and attributing negative outcomes to external causes

Communication, like power and leadership, is a capacity with no inherent morality. It is up to the user to apply it ethically.

# Lesson

Be clear and consistent when communicating. Don't assume that everyone will understand the nuances in your language. The trick "shake" to one dog might be called "paw" to another. Just because there wasn't the desired response to one command doesn't mean that the dog doesn't know the trick—he may just know it under another name. Also, beware of people who are really great communicators and therefore excel in impression management. The more talented one is at communicating, the more potential damage he can do if he puts those talents toward unethical ends.

# 40

Answers without Questions

*Balancing theory and practice*

10152045. What does it mean to you?

Probably nothing. In and of itself it is just a random sequence of numbers. Notice how the meaning changes when I tell you it's an answer to a question. If it's the answer to the question "What date will social security funds run out?" (10/15/2045), all of a sudden those neutral numbers become depressing. However, if it's the correct answer to "What are tomorrow's winning lottery numbers?" (10-1-5-20-4-5), those numbers become very exciting! Answers without questions mean nothing, yet this is the prevalent way that people approach learning.

I took five years off between college and business school, and I worked all kinds of jobs at all different levels (actually, I took another five between my MBA and my MSL, or master's in leadership, too). What I learned by getting my hands dirty and seeing how businesses are really run was invaluable. When I arrived at Tulane, this experience translated into perspective and questions that made the classes much more useful. I felt like I came away with much more than some of my classmates who entered grad school directly from college.[111] The difference is theory (the world of answers) versus reality (a world of questions). College and grad school are mostly concerned with theory, so without a break in between the two, it's easy to believe that that theory is reality. It's only when you're out in the world with your advanced degree that you learn the world doesn't fit nicely in a tidy concept. By then you've missed your opportunity to get all those "real world" questions answered in class. Put simply, you have to have the questions before the answers make sense.

The best learning is a search for answers. Working experience is about being confronted with questions that you may not know the answer to. Going to work gives you substantial experience, questions, and perspective that then provide the basis for true personal advancement when you seek and find the answer. Education is not about the *possession* of knowledge; it's the experience of *putting forth the effort to obtain* it.

We've been told that if we want to train our dogs out of a bad behavior, we have to catch them in the act. Even a few moments later and they won't know why they're being reprimanded. It's been too long between the event and the consequence, and there's no connection between the two anymore. It's almost possible to see the expression of *Ok, I know I did something wrong, but what?* on their faces. Telling them "Bad dog!" after the fact is merely an answer hanging out there with no question to give it meaning. I'm effectively telling yelling "10152045!" at them. They can guess that it's bad, but there's

---

[111] Of course, I don't know this to be actually true at all. It's just a feeling. How would you even measure such a thing?

no real learning going on, no association with a question such as *I wonder how they'll react if I dig through the kitchen trash and look for treats?*

Training the dogs involves constant vacillation between lesson and application. Zeke may learn not to jump on us in the house, but when he's overwhelmed with excitement and in a different environment at my uncle's house he soon forgets. Over time we make gradual progress. It's a back-and-forth exercise where Zeke "questions" where the boundaries of no jumping are, and I tell him. *Can I jump on you?* No. *Can I jump on her?* No. *Can I jump on you outside the house?* No. *Can I jump on that stranger?* No. *Can I jump on that other stranger?* No. *Can I jump on someone at the park?* No. Eventually, by trial and error, he learns that what I really meant all along was no jumping on anyone, anywhere, ever.[112]

---

[112] Unless someone breaks in. Then jump on them. And bite them.

suggest that the challenge is to examine our conscious-
ness for those ways in which we leaders may project more
shadow than light...the problem is that people tend to rise
to leadership in our society by a tendency toward extrover-
sion, which too often means ignoring what's going on inside
themselves...I have looked at some training programs for
leaders, and I am discouraged by how often they focus on
the development of skills to manipulate the external world
rather than the skills necessary to go within and make the
spiritual journey...It feeds a dangerous syndrome among
leaders who already tend to deny their inner world.[113]

We'll look at life as a canoe ride, why it's so difficult to use a pointed finger
to show a dog something, and the power of three. In addition we'll examine
why people in older, cheaper cars might look happier and why some bosses
treat their employees as if they were on shock collars.

Finally, we'll look at the importance of taking time to find out who
you are and getting comfortable with it, and also the importance of simply
throwing a ball with your dog.

[113] Palmer 1994

# 41

# The Canoe

*Leading your life with a light touch*

The other day my wife told me that the children's song "Row, row, row your boat" is actually a yogic mantra. It apparently is used as a metaphor to describe how one should approach life. A soft touch is needed, so that "your boat" is handled "gently" and you can continue on "merrily, merrily, merrily, merrily," because after all, "life is but a dream." I'm not sure if this is the true origin, but it certainly makes you think.

Life certainly can be seen as a current or flow that we are all caught up in. At times it's swift and dangerous, and other times it's smooth and even. We all sit in our little canoes being carried downstream. This metaphor is ingrained in our common psyche, as evidenced by our colloquialisms.

Someone is "swimming upstream" or "fighting against the current" when they choose to oppose the majority. Being betrayed means we were "sold down the river." When we are in real trouble we are "up the creek without a paddle."

My own approach to life is also best summed up using this theme. As I see it, we are all given paddles to navigate our personal canoes down the stream of life. There is a certain range of action we can take, but we are also caught up in the flow and can only do so much about it. Obstacles exist along the way that we want to avoid. Shallow water may ground us for a while, keeping us from making any forward progress until we find a way to dislodge ourselves. Rocks or downed trees may lie in our path threatening to bruise, batter, or even sink us. The current may be fast or leisurely, the depth of the river deep or shallow.

Through it all we have our little paddle. We can spend all our time vigilant, rowing vigorously and using up all of our energy trying to stay *exactly* where we think we should be in the stream—but this is exhausting. Imagine trying to keep a canoe within inches of where you want it as you are carried down a stream. It's impossible. The current will constantly throw you off. But there are people who live their lives in just this way—constantly worrying and expending energy to ensure that they are exactly where they believe they should be. Any time they are thrown off course by the current of life they become stressed and fight like cornered cats to get back to where they want to be.

On the other hand there are those of us who don't use the paddle at all. These people have *total* faith in the flow of the stream. They lie back in the canoe staring up at the sun as it peeks through the canopy of trees. This isn't too wise either. While they are conserving their energy, they are taking no precautions against inevitable obstacles. Sooner or later they are beached on a riverbank, caught up in the branches of a fallen tree, or maybe even capsized.

The best approach is relaxed awareness.[114] Use your paddle when you need to, but pull it in when you don't. Have a little faith that the current of life will take you generally in a good direction, but make an effort to steer your little vessel away from trouble and in a desirable direction. Don't stress if you are not exactly where you intended to be. Paddle a bit when you don't like where you are going. Know that there will be times of calm and times of rough water. If you are whitewater rafting, have faith that the river will widen and calm before too long. But when you need to, do whatever it takes to stay upright and afloat.[115]

Drawing a parallel to leadership isn't difficult. Like it or not, we are all leading our own lives. The lesson doesn't change when we lead others. Micromanagers and control freaks make poor leaders, as they don't give their followers any space or breathing room. They tend to view their employees as machines that are there to perform their functions perfectly, and that's it. On the other side of the spectrum are managers who give no structure or guidance at all. Whether it's due to fear, lack of ability, apathy, or overconfidence, they stay completely out of the picture. Effective leadership finds a balance between the two extremes, where the most productive level of interaction depends on the followers and the situation. For instance, professionally trained doctors working in a research lab may need less oversight than entry-level employees working in fast food. If the situation is routine and familiar (the same work is done in the same way everyday), then less oversight is needed.

In the chapter "Just Jump In," I described how Paco goes berserk when he's in a canoe, propelling himself into worse and worse situations through panic. Zeke is calm as a cucumber and would probably snooze his way over a waterfall. By adopting a middle-of-the-road strategy, you can obtain the best outcomes while conserving your energy for when it is important. Most importantly, it should be a long and enjoyable ride.

---

[114] This is like the Buddhist concept of mindfulness.
[115] A similar concept is that of the cornered cat. Most of the time cats are relaxed and aloof and seem to take life in stride. When they are cornered, they drop this approach and fight like hell.

# Lesson

Remember what you learned in kindergarten: Row gently down the stream and make every attempt to stay merry. Keep an eye out to see where the current of life is taking you, and paddle accordingly. Try to avoid demanding that you be in one exact location, and have a little faith in the flow. But stay alert and don't doze on your way down, or you may end up high and dry or capsized.

# 42

🦴

# The Power of Presence
*Raising awareness just by being there*

Paco can be a jealous dog. Every time I give Michaele a hug in his presence he yips and barks at me. *Hey, that's* my *little monkey!* (We joke that he sees us as monkeys—I'm Big Monkey, she's Little Monkey.) If I'm in the right mood I tease him. *"My* Michaele," I'll say, goading him on to fits.

Even if we aren't hugging, Paco stares. He sits in the corner and watches us talk. I think he just wants to be included. Once we notice, it's hard to continue the conversation. Suddenly we are aware of ourselves. The feeling is similar to when there is feedback on the phone line and you hear your own voice a second after speaking. He's a third presence, and our one-to-one dynamic is broken by his stare and our knowledge that we are being viewed from a third point of view.

The number three has always held a certain power in human culture. The Holy Trinity, body, mind, and spirit, and past, present, and future are some foundational applications of three. There are many theories on why the number three carries so much symbolic weight. Only with the presence of a third is perspective gained between unity and duality. One element has nothing to compare itself to, two elements provide awareness of one another, but only with the addition of the third is the perspective of the interrelationship between the individuals recognized as existing in itself:

One by itself has no perspective.

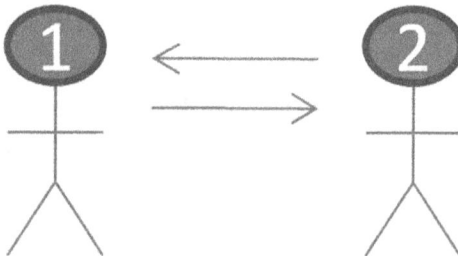

Two are aware of each other.

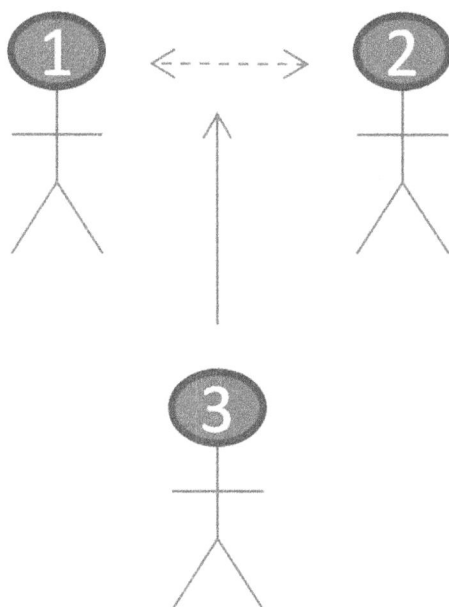

A third sees the interaction as a thing in itself,
the beginning of deeper perspective.

At three both the integrity of the individual elements and the interdependence of each on all the others becomes manifest. Put simply, when you
are in a discussion with one other person, usually you are lost in the conversation itself. But when you know you are being observed discussing, then that
discussion becomes a thing in itself.

This applies to leadership on two levels. First, an effective leader is like
person #3 above—they are aware of the interrelationship between others and
manage that as much as they manage the people themselves. This pulls the
focus away from unproductive competitive thinking ("me versus him") and
toward collective efforts toward a third element such as a goal.

Second, every concept in leadership directly relates to this balance
between individual integrity and interdependence of all elements. A leader
is one who must balance techniques to improve himself as an individual

with the effectiveness of interacting with others. Not only does he contribute directly with his talents, "his characteristics constitute a set of resources contributing to the effective utilization of other resources."[116] By fulfilling this third-party role, a leader becomes a mechanism through which the resources of the other two participants become more productive; the whole becomes more than the sum of the parts.

However, with too much focus on either extreme leadership becomes ineffective. A leader who is too self-involved and narcissistic is not effective, but neither is a leader who focuses completely on followers and ignores her own self-development.

---

[116] Pierce and Newstrom 2008

# Lesson

Just as Paco makes Michaele and me self-conscious when he stares at us, a leader brings a third element, an outside perspective, to the interactions of employees. The introduction of this point of view increases the productivity and quality of interaction between all elements. All parties become more aware of the relationships between each other, and between themselves and their work. Leadership involves the knowledge of the interaction of all pieces, not just self, not just other, not just other-to-other. By recognizing not only individuals (themselves included), but the interplay between everyone, a leader may better work through challenges to accomplish common objectives. In the process, he contributes to the overall more productive use of available resources.

# 43

$\bowtie$

# You Can't Use Shock Collars in the Office

*Leadership versus dominance*

It's easy to be dominant over a dog. A trainer even taught us "dominance positions" to send a clear message that we are in control. When Zeke challenged me with a growl in his early years,[117] I would stand over him, and then essentially lie on him, knees tucked under my belly and my chin resting on his head. There we'd sit for a minute or two, me holding him in a person-box. *I'm the boss here. Remember that.*

To teach them basic obedience we got zapper collars. In apartment life you make more friends when you can keep your dogs from barking at every noise and

---

[117] I guess this is kind of like a teenager talking back.

jumping up on strangers. The collars were intended as training aids for sporting dogs. Since poor Paco never got to fulfill his calling of herding cattle, we used them as gentle reminders to listen to us. The remote controls had black knobs where the intensity could be controlled. Our trainer told us that we needed to test them out on ourselves first to know what setting was comfortable. Of course, I was the first guinea pig. Michaele gleefully started on setting one as I held the two prongs of the device to my palm. She pressed the button. Nothing. Up to two. Nothing. Three...four...no shock. There are only eight options, so I was beginning to think something was broken. Finally on five it struck, and I jumped off the couch, instinctively throwing it across the room. The idea was to slowly build up to tolerance. So much for that! The shock was so intense I responded as if someone had dropped a dictionary on the wood floor right behind me. As soon as it began, it was over. Once we figured out how to use the collars at a much lower setting, they were for the most part effective with the dogs—until they figured out that no collar means no shock. We've reached a compromise: we don't use the collars anymore and they listen to us most of the time.

Dominance is easy. If you have more power, and use it to your advantage, you're dominant. But leadership should not be confused with the simple use of power. Force may get results when you're present, but as soon as your back is turned, it unravels. Newton's third law of motion backs us up on this one. In the following excerpt of the law, I've taken the "F" that stands for force and replaced it with "FU," a common sentiment toward bad leaders. Let's see how true it is:

> The mutual forces of action and reaction between two bodies are equal, opposite, and collinear. This means that whenever a first body exerts a force *FU* on a second body, the second body exerts a force *-FU* on the first body. *FU* and *-FU* are equal in magnitude and opposite in direction. This law is sometimes referred to as the action- reaction law, with *FU* called the "action" and *-FU* the "reaction." The action and the reaction are simultaneous.[118]

---

[118] Newton 1729

Almost three hundred years ago we already knew that every FU produces another simultaneous FU equal in magnitude, directed right back at the source of the first! We didn't even need the invention of bad managers.

The boss, parent, or condo association president who rules solely with dominance produces a tidal wave of resentment that will wash them away sooner or later. Force and firmness have their place, and sometimes leaders need to use these tactics, but always with the knowledge that there is no better alternative and that there will be an equal and opposite reaction.

In a meta-study of the effectiveness of leader behaviors, four dimensions emerged that might be considered the pillars of effective leader behavior.[119] The more of them a leader embodies, the better the leader tends to be. As you read through them below, ask yourself how many of these behaviors require force and dominance:

1. **Support**: Behavior that enhances someone else's feeling of personal worth and importance.

2. **Interaction facilitation**: Behavior that encourages members of the group to develop close, mutually satisfying relationships.

3. **Goal emphasis**: Behavior that stimulates an enthusiasm for meeting the group's goal or achieving excellent performance.

4. **Work facilitation**: Behavior that helps achieve goal attainment by such activities as scheduling, coordinating, planning, and by providing resources such as tools, materials, and technical knowledge.

True leaders recognize that they represent and channel the energies of the people, but they aren't ever a replacement for them. Alexandre Auguste Ledru-Rollin, a nineteenth-century French politician, said, "There go the people. I must follow them for I am their leader."[120]

---

[119] Bowers and Seashore 1966
[120] Ledru-Rollin 2002

# Lesson

Don't confuse dominance with leadership. Simply using brute force—whether physical, verbal, or psychological—is an ill-advised and short-term strategy. It almost always ends in a backlash and the unraveling of efforts of the leader. In many cases it results in a pendulum swing in the exact opposite direction. Forced change isn't real change. Think of the dogs—the effectiveness of our dominant approach quickly wore off and we settled into a productive common understanding over time.

# 44

The Richest Dog Doesn't
Have a Dime

*Wisdom and grace as measures of wealth*

Ok, right off the bat, I know some of you are thinking, "Wait! There are some seriously rich dogs out there. What about Trouble, Leona Helmsley's Maltese who inherited $12 million?" I know. But did the dog know she was rich?

When I was on long-haul road trips back and forth from school there was a game I used to play to pass the time. I'd compare the expressions of the people driving by to the value of their cars. It was a simple thing, but revealing. In general, there was a direct inverse proportion between the two.

The more expensive the car, the more unhappy the driver would look. Young kids would zip by in old Toyotas with the windows down, singing with their friends. Behind them a somber BMW driver would sit, mouth set tightly and eyes straight ahead. When's the last time you saw someone in a newer Mercedes singing out loud behind the wheel?

I also noticed that there was a slightly higher chance that the wealthy people were alone in the car. If they did have passengers, they also looked generally unamused. Why is this? When I told others about my observations, they offered up all kinds of explanations. The more responsible people have more money. The luxury cars come with big monthly payments that provide constant stress. Those with cheaper cars tend to be younger and more carefree. But I've noticed that age doesn't really make that much of a difference. Whatever the reason, I knew which car I'd rather be in.[121]

It got me to thinking which group I'd rather be part of in general. To paraphrase Billy Joel, I'd rather laugh with the middle than cry with the rich (or if you prefer rap, the Notorious B.I.G. reminded us, "Mo' money, mo' problems").[122] But what does this mean? How could less money be more attractive? Of course, the answer is that it isn't about the money at all. It's about another measure of wealth: enjoyment of life. Maybe all those luxury-car owners were out of balance, cashing in all their energy and spare time just to climb the status ladder.

Maybe the time has come to focus on what brings true happiness: wisdom, grace, family, friends, and doing right by other people. I saw a T-shirt recently in a San Francisco bookstore that proclaimed, "You don't have to f\*\*k over other people to succeed in life," and I thought *Yeah! That's right!* There's nothing wrong with wealth or acquisition of material

---

[121] And yes, I know the difference between correlation and causation. I'm aware this is just an observed correlation and a whole bunch of speculation.
[122] Of course, there are many wealthy people who live balanced, contented, and happy lives, just as there are many miserable people in the middle.

things so long as it isn't the sole purpose of life. Having doesn't always require taking.[123]

A good friend of mine who is a professor of oceanography has long been railing against Keynesian economics. He faults the approach for being too short-sighted both upstream and downstream, and not taking into account the full costs of acquiring raw materials and disposing of products post-use. For example, consider the cost of palm oil. Traditional economics would include the cost of harvesting the palms, processing them, transporting the oil, packaging it, and distributing it. From all of these an appropriate price is determined, considering profit.

But there's more to it than that. What are the costs of destroying orangutan habitats to plant palms? Of taking over native land and changing the ecosystem? Where do the processed palm solids go? Is there an environmental cost to disposal of the solids or the used oil? A true cost of the product incorporates impacts farther up and down the value stream.

What happens if we apply this same line of thought to the acquisition of money? We know our time is worth money. We're willing to give it up for a certain price. Some people will work a hundred hours a week for $100,000 a year, while others would rather work forty hours a week for $50,000. Effort is also typically considered when weighing what's worth earning. We expect to be paid more for ten hours of hard work than ten hours of leisurely work. A third factor is risk. The more dangerous a job is, the higher the pay, generally (holding constant the factor of expertise). From a traditional perspective, we choose the benefit of acquiring wealth by considering the time, effort, and risk involved in the effort to obtain it. Brain surgeons are very well paid, but most of us decide it isn't worth the school, time, expense, and effort to become one.

Unfortunately we're not such simple creatures. How much is time away from family worth? Is a day of travel for the single man the same cost as for

---

[123] For instance, see *Gain Power by Giving it Away* chapter.

a father of four? What about psychological factors? Is the routine of sitting in a chair in a windowless beige office for eight hours the same as working outside in an ocean-side park on a sunny day for eight hours? And consider opportunity cost.[124] Is the insurance salesman who wanted to be a chef paying a higher price for every day of work than the guy who actually wanted to be an insurance salesman?

Think about how most dogs live their lives. They are some of the most naturally happy and carefree beings around. How much acquiring and stockpiling of stuff do they do? We can't all live off of love and goodwill, but look to the model of your dog when you determine how best to spend your days. Louis Saban must have known this when he said, "No matter how much money and how few possessions you own, having a dog makes you rich."[125]

---

[124] Opportunity cost is the value given up by doing one thing over another. For example, staying home for an unpaid sick day isn't free—it costs me the money I would have earned if I had gone to work.
[125] Saban 2007

# Lesson

Consider all impacts on your life when you run after wealth for wealth's sake. Make an informed decision. Long ago I was told, "Making a lot of money is easy as long as it's the only thing you want to do." If you want to live a balanced life, it may be a little more challenging. Consider what really makes you happy, where true enjoyment comes from. If a shiny new Ferrari is the most coveted thing in your life, go for it, but if you decide to spend more time with your wife and kids than your coworkers, don't feel like you are falling behind in the race to keep up with the Joneses. When they separate and go through a messy divorce because he was never around, it won't matter what kind of car he drives to his divorce lawyer's office.

# 45

# Paco Now Eats Carrots

*Chasing other people's desires is a waste of time*

I've always been a car person. Ever since my first old beater car when I was sixteen I switched cars every few years. For a while it didn't matter the make or model, I just enjoyed driving all of the different kinds. At one point, shortly after graduating from college, I traded in my sporty Toyota Celica for a bright orange 1973 VW van complete with a pop-up camper top and a sink. That one didn't last long as my dreams of taking it cross-country met the reality that it could barely make it to the corner store to get a gallon of milk.

Over the years I started getting fancier and fancier cars, culminating in a pristine Jaguar S-type a few years ago.[126] I had gotten wrapped up in the image of the cars somewhere along the way and had lost that feeling of fun that I used to have with them. At the time my wife was commuting a ways to work, so we switched cars for a few weeks. When realized that I got just as much pleasure from driving my high-mileage older Subaru as my snazzy Jaguar, I resolved to get back to what *I* wanted to drive and not just what looked good to others. I traded in the Jaguar for another Subaru.

Both the Subarus went into storage when we moved to Europe for a year. The idea was to be carless for the year, but my motor-head passions rose up and I found a high-mileage twelve-year-old VW Golf diesel for a good price. This car was truly basic. Not only was it lacking air-conditioning but the windows were still operated by hand with a crank. I hadn't seen manual windows in years. In addition to the dozen years of wear in the interior, the car's diesel engine sounded like a giant sewing machine going down the road.

I knew the car was only temporary, but still there was an adjustment as I was confronted with my own snobbery. Then a funny thing happened. After driving the car for a month, I didn't care anymore about any of its "shortcomings." It was a reliable car, got me from point A to point B, and nothing else mattered. I started thinking about all the time, money, and effort I had put into getting nicer and nicer cars over the years. Was it a waste? Why did it matter what others thought? How did I get sidetracked from pursuing what I wanted (simply the joy of driving) to pursuing what I had been told was important (luxury and status cars)? I must have enjoyed the attention from driving the nicer cars, because otherwise there was no reason for me to have them.

I started thinking about how much enjoyment of things requires someone else wanting what you have. For better or worse, much of human motivation has to do with having that desirable item and enjoying the status that other people's jealousy or interest gives you. Whether it is the larger house,

---

[126] If you want to see a car that loses value fast, look at Jaguars. This car had thirteen thousand miles on it and cost me about one-third of the original price.

the luxury car, or the promotion at work, a majority of the satisfaction of having the new thing comes from what others think about it and about you with it. When that fades, as it always does over time, then you are left with hoping that you enjoy it for its own sake.

Wanting something because another does is so instinctual it even happens with the dogs. Zeke will take a treat and put it aside for hours, sitting near to it but not touching it and sometimes even napping next to it, until Paco begins to get jealous. Then, when a sufficient amount of jealousy has built up, Zeke will make a big show of enjoying it immensely, making sure that Paco is watching him. He even does this with us. If we take Paco out for a walk and leave Zeke at home we usually give Zeke a treat to occupy him. He will wait until we get back to touch it. Clearly in these instances it simply is not enjoyable unless someone else is witnessing him eat it.

A few months ago I started tossing the dogs the fat ends of carrots that I cut up. I figured Paco is such a garbage mouth that he would surely gobble them up. Oddly, he spat them out, and picky old Zeke crunched them all up. Paco, watching Zeke enjoy his carrot nubs, began to think maybe he's missing something and tried to give them another try. He now eats them but it's clear he still thinks they taste terrible. Every attempt evinces a wince and a twisted up mouth. You can practically hear him think, *"Bleccchh! This is horrible!"* He keeps eating them, just because Zeke likes them. He can't stand to think that Zeke is getting his unfair share of anything, even something nasty, so he chokes them down.

Seeing this behavior so blatantly in the dogs drove home the point to me that we rethink what is actually important to us and what only seems important because it's important to someone else. It is very easy to fall into the trap of chasing goals that only provide the benefit of other people's praise. While getting the jealousy and attention of others may be a good reason to go after something (like a nice car), they soon fade. When they do, usually all that's left is the negative consequences of going after the goal (for instance, the car payment).

This type of behavior is true followership. You are following what others (the media, your social circle) tell you is important, and not defining for yourself what is truly important to you. Deciding independently, and with full knowledge of what factors are influencing your decisions, is an important step toward developing your leadership skills.

Much of this comes down to self-confidence, a trait highly correlated with effective leaders.[127] By constantly chasing what others have defined as important, you are not sorting through the information to decide for yourself (remember that when you surrender your ability to define your own reality, you surrender power to another). Life is especially uncertain for leaders:

> A great deal of information must be processed. A constant series of problems must be solved and decisions made. Followers have to be convinced to pursue specific courses of action. Setbacks have to be overcome. Competing interest have to be satisfied. Risks have to be taken in the face of uncertainty. A person riddled with self-doubt would never be able to take the necessary actions nor command the respect of others.[128]

Isn't chasing other people's goals a form of self-doubt? *Maybe I'm driving the wrong car. Maybe my refrigerator isn't good enough. Maybe people will think more of me if I make VP.*

If my wife and I had taken everyone else's advice on what breed of dog to adopt, we most likely would not have adopted either Paco or Zeke. Blue heelers and pit bulls are two of the most abandoned breeds of dogs. They clearly are not very highly valued by others in general as they are dropped off at shelters, left on the side of the road, or worse. We value and love these dogs because of who they are and not because of the perception of others. Something has value because *you* determine it has value, not because other people say it does.

---

[127] Kirkpatrick and Locke 1991
[128] ibid.

# Lesson

Don't waste time going after what other people want or chasing other people's expectations or goals for you. Define your own and make sure that they have a benefit to you other than just how they appear to others. It's difficult in this world of media overload to figure out what you actually want and what you are just told you should want, but make the effort to chart your own path. Lead yourself toward your own unique and meaningful goals. Remember that when you let others tell you what goals to go after, you are letting them define your reality for you, and in the process you're giving them power over you.

# 46

**❧**

# Chewing Gum Saves Lives
*Creating space in the midst of panic and hurry*

Years ago I had a client who owned a small airport. He offered a flight school, firefighting services, plane storage and avionics repairs, and a flight shop. When I was interviewing the general manager, who was also an accomplished pilot, I asked him if he'd ever had an emergency while on a solo flight. "Sure," he told me. When I asked him what happened, he responded that the single engine just cut out when he was at about ten thousand feet. He was all alone, and the plane started to go down. I'm not a big fan of flying, so the story was especially captivating, as it played out my worst fears. I asked, "So what did you do?"

"Well," he responded, "I reached into my shirt pocket and took out the pack of Juicy Fruit gum I always keep there." He looked at me.

"*And?*" I asked, on the edge of my seat.

"And then I took out a stick of gum, removed the foil wrapping, and put the piece into my mouth."

"But what about the plane?"

"Oh, it was going down at this point," he assured me. "I chewed my gum for a few seconds, thought about my options, chose the best course of action, and followed it."

"That makes sense, but why in the world did you need a piece of gum right then?" I asked.

"Well, taking that gum out, unwrapping it, and chewing it for a moment gave me a chance to gather my thoughts and make sure I was not just panicking, but choosing the best option. What I lost in time then more than made up for it when I knew I was making the right decision on how to best correct the situation safely."[129]

I was stunned. Who thinks to casually unwrap some gum to chew when their plane is going down? But it did make sense. Those extra few "wasted" minutes were vital to his safety, as it kept him from just doing *anything* (and probably the wrong thing) when the crisis hit. He had created space to do nothing in the midst of a situation that demanded he do something and was better off for it.

One of the hardest things to do is nothing. Try it. Actually, if you are trying to do nothing, then you aren't really doing nothing—you are trying. In our increasingly busy lives, we never schedule the time to do nothing. If

---

[129] It turns out the right thing to do was to steer the plane into the dive to build up speed, and then to level off nearer the ground and glide to a safe touchdown from a low altitude. This brings up another philosophical issue: when is it safer to steer *into* the danger than away from it?

we schedule downtime it usually is taken up by an activity—reading, watching TV, or sleeping. My dogs spend the better part of their days dozing and lazing around. Of course this isn't possible for most of us, but giving yourself even ten (ideally fifteen to thirty) minutes a day to just *be* can be very beneficial. It serves as a time to get perspective and energy.

I try to meditate every day. Usually I fail, and I end up spending my extra time in some frivolous activity like surfing the net. The times that I do get to meditate are wonderful. Recently I began to take on a few more clients. This happened just as my last classes at Boston University were heading into finals and my wife started a new job. Things got hectic really quickly. When I finally found a chance to simply sit and focus on my breathing, I could actually feel the clutter in my mind start to settle. It was like a Tetris game where all the pieces are poorly placed and new ones keep dropping quickly from above. When my "screen" (my mind) was almost filled to the top, things finally started to fit together. With each minute I sat quietly another piece fell perfectly into place, reducing the chaos and creating space in my mind for new information and peaceful reflection.

Not long ago a friend of mine introduced me to a small start-up company she had heard of. It's a brilliant idea. The company sells T-shirts and asks the purchaser to commit to ten minutes of helping others each day the shirt is worn. Each morning that the shirt comes out of the drawer in the morning, the wearer makes a mental promise to find ten minutes in the day for the benefit of others. The idea (and the business) is based on the fact that the idea will spread with others buying a shirt and making the same conscious choice to help. Knowing how beneficial it is for me to take a few minutes of each day to meditate, I thought of co-opting the idea for a company called Take 30. The wearer of this T-shirt would commit to spending half an hour of his day doing *nothing*. It could be meditating, lying on the couch staring up at the ceiling in silence, or sitting in the car at the beach with the radio off looking out at the surf. The rule would be that during those thirty minutes, you could not sleep, watch anything that ran on electricity, or interact with any other person (or pet). You could not actively pursue any goal other than just being.

There is so much we don't know about ourselves, and we look everywhere outside for it. We soak up information, get advanced degrees, pursue our careers, buy things, and build relationships. Yet, we don't look inside. Aside from being a useful way to step out of the fray in order to better handle it when you step back in, the simple exercise of doing nothing is a first step to getting familiar with yourself.

It's difficult enough to lead others effectively. If you don't have a decent knowledge of yourself, it's almost impossible. I had a friend a few years back who had all the characteristics of attention deficit disorder. (I don't know whether or not she had been diagnosed.) Sweet as she was, she would run around all day frantically putting out fires (real and imagined) and following her active and worried mind. I asked her once what she would do if she was forced to sit down quietly with herself in a room with no distractions. She told me she would probably explode. Maybe she would have needed more than a T-shirt.

# Lesson

Make an effort to create space for nothingness, especially when you feel that you absolutely have no time to. It's then that you may get the most benefit out of some perspective. The time you "lose" doing nothing will come back to you many times over in the better decisions you make as a result of your perspective. Take 30. Sit down quietly with no objective a few times a week and spend time with yourself without distraction. Let whatever happens happen, but don't pursue any goal. Just be. You should slowly start to gain perspective on yourself. Your mind may settle a bit, and you may see things slightly differently. This is the first step to effectively leading others, as you are better able to know yourself. When crises hit, observe them first and then consider your options instead of just instinctively reacting to them.

# 47

こーつ

# Hooray for the Packaging
*Finding value in the mundane*

I've found my dogs' crazy button. It makes them snap from asleep to hysterical faster than the mailman sticking a fat catalog through the mail slot. What's their drug? Bubble wrap. They especially love the kind that consists of large pockets of air about the size of a soda can but really any kind will do.

It may have started when I tauntingly popped it in Zeke's face one day. Maybe I tapped into some primal "dog versus packaged air" animosity. It doesn't make any sense, but it sure is hilarious—and dangerous. This game is not for the faint of heart. I have to be careful to remember that they have this affliction, or I'm caught off guard. Say I get a book in the mail, and upon opening it I casually (and forgetfully) pick out the air packs. Within two seconds Zeke snaps like an alligator at my hand. Paco vaults vertically in the air to mid-chest height, lunging at the plastic prey. At this point the new purchase is on the ground, and I'm fending them off with elbows and shouts. Of course I am partially to blame for all this, but it doesn't mean that I'm always in the mood for an attack.

If it wasn't so alarming it'd be entertaining. They don't relent until I show the empty box and tell them there are no more, all gone! Shreds of plastic litter the floor. Exhausted, they collapse and drift off to a blissful sleep. The threat is overcome. *One more victory in the battle against the plastic popping army.*

No other toy gives them this much extreme pleasure. They remind me of the child who's given an expensive toboggan for Christmas and spends the day playing in the box it came in. In fact, the few times we have given them gifts under the Christmas tree, they too enjoy the wrapping as much as the toy itself.

Paco's favorite toy is a fleece blanket. We discovered that a four dollar cheap throw from the drug store is a greater source of amusement than a twenty dollar trinket at a specialty pet store. There is simply no substitute for this odd preference.

We should all be so lucky to find value in the mundane. Who says a new car is better than your existing one, if it brings a smile to your face with reminders of good times? Isn't a coffee cup that has been in your family more valuable than a replacement picked up at a pottery store?

There's nothing wrong with preferring fancy gadgets and clothes. Often new is better, but this is not always the case. Consider BMW and Mercedes— both brands have dropped in quality ratings in the past years. Your four-year-old Honda may be a better car than a new Bimmer. The dogs have reminded me to look honestly at what I have and what I think I want. Am I replacing something just for the sake of change? What do I truly value and what do I only think I need?

I've heard it said that clothes fit best when you aren't even aware they are there. This is the case with leaders as well. Lao Tzu reminded us that, "A leader is best when people barely know he exists; when his work is done, his aim fulfilled, they will say: we did it ourselves." Even BB King advises us that, "You don't miss your water until your well runs dry." Similarly, perhaps the best in our lives consists of what is under the radar, what we don't notice. These are the mundane parts of life: the boxes, the bubble wrap, the packaging. And the mundane is what makes all the new things look extra shiny in contrast. The dogs are a constant reminder that something as boring as waking up in the morning can be an event to celebrate if you look at it the right way.

# Lesson

Reconsider the mundane in your life—the space in between. Just as the best leader is one whose followers barely know he exists, some of the best aspects of our lives are the small, plain, and background parts. Find contentment in the little things that make you happy, such as your morning cup of coffee or your favorite song coming on the radio.

# 48

Finger at the Moon

*Looking past what is said to what is meant*

O ver fifty years ago a social scientist argued that there is a far more important function of a leader than merely mobilizing support for his initiatives and keeping the organization running smoothly. The primary function of a leader, he argued, is to "define the ends of group existence, to design an enterprise distinctively adapted to these ends, and to see that design become a living reality."[130] One challenge then, is to communicate these "ends of group existence" to others. A leader needs to convey to others where he wants to go, what the vision for the company is, and how to get there. The problem is that not everyone will understand.

---

[130] Selznick 1957

When I want to show Paco where his toy is, I point to it. "Paco," I'll say, "where's your blanket? Go get your blanket!" He'll usually follow in the direction I've pointed and quickly find it. When I try this technique on Zeke, he just stares at the tip of my pointed finger. He doesn't understand that the finger indicates something greater: a direction. Zeke's mind just can't make that mental leap.

There's an old story in Buddhism about trying to define truth. Truth, the story goes, is like the moon. The wise old sage may point to the moon in an attempt to describe it to the seeker, but most seekers end up just looking at the sage's finger itself, never realizing that it is in fact pointing at the moon. The Sixth Patriarch Huineng, a Zen monk born in China in 638 and widely considered to be one of the most important figures in Buddhism, tells us that, "Truth has nothing to do with words. Truth can be likened to the bright moon in the sky. Words, in this case, can be likened to a finger. The finger can point to the moon's location. However, the finger is not the moon. To look at the moon, it is necessary to gaze beyond the finger, right?"[131]

What does this mean? It means that most people, despite their best intentions in trying to learn more and reach higher levels of understanding, often get tied up with concepts, definitions, and descriptions (the pointing finger), without ever making the leap of comprehension to the bigger realization (the moon itself). They make tremendous effort to collect information about the finger but never look beyond to actually see the moon.

Happiness, like truth, is one of these concepts that there is much discussion and interest about but one which few people really "get" in a visceral way, despite lots of good intentions and study. Steve Hagen, in his phenomenal book *Buddhism Plain and Simple,*[132] uses a visual aid to help make a point about forgetting the details once you learn them so that you can more easily "get" the bigger picture. He uses a black and white image, and asks you to "see the cow" in the picture (to have a look at the cow yourself, visit Steve's

---

[131] unknown, Finger Pointing at the Moon 2007
[132] Hagen 1998

website[133]). Hagen explains that there is only so much describing one can do to help another see the cow; at a certain point one has to just see it on his or her own. They have to understand themselves in order to go from a pattern of black and white on the page to the clear image of a cow, to go from the finger pointing at the moon to seeing the moon itself.

One simple example of mixing up the finger and the moon is the pursuit of a fancy car. Before credit, only the wealthy could afford luxury cars, and so these vehicles (the finger) indicated personal wealth (the moon). As credit became widely available, average people could acquire a Mercedes or Land Rover. In doing so, they took out loans they may not have been able to afford. The act of attaining the car (the finger, or symbol of wealth) took them farther away from the actual goal: personal wealth. By confusing the finger with the moon we make foolish decisions or simply get lost.

There's a well-known story of a consultant and a fisherman. The original author is unknown, but the following version can be found online:[134]

> A management consultant, on holiday in an African fishing village, watched a little fishing boat dock at the quayside. Noting the quality of the fish, the consultant asked the fisherman how long it had taken to catch them.
>
> "Not very long," answered the fisherman.
>
> "Then, why didn't you stay out longer and catch more?" asked the consultant.
>
> The fisherman explained that his small catch was sufficient to meet his needs and those of his family.
>
> The consultant asked, "But what do you do with the rest of your time?"

[133] http://www.dharmafield.org/ If you cannot find the image there, simply Google "Steve Hagen Cow"
[134] unknown, The Consultant and the Fisherman 2011

"I sleep late, fish a little, play with my children, and have an afternoon's rest under a coconut tree. In the evenings, I go into the community hall to see my friends, have a few beers, play the drums, and sing a few songs...I have a full and happy life," replied the fisherman.

The consultant ventured, "I have an MBA from Harvard, and I can help you. You should start by fishing longer every day. You can then sell the extra fish you catch. With the extra revenue, you can buy a bigger boat. With the extra money the larger boat will bring, you can buy a second one and a third one and so on until you have a large fleet. Instead of selling your fish to a middleman, you can negotiate directly with the processing plants and maybe even open your own plant. You can then leave this little village and move to a city here or maybe even in the United Kingdom, from where you can direct your huge enterprise."

"How long would that take?" asked the fisherman.

"Oh, ten, maybe twenty years," replied the consultant.

"And after that?" asked the fisherman.

"After that? That's when it gets really interesting," answered the consultant, laughing. "When your business gets really big, you can start selling shares in your company and make millions!"

"Millions? Really? And after that?" pressed the fisherman.

"After that you'll be able to retire, move out to a small village by the sea, sleep in late every day, spend time with your family, go fishing, take afternoon naps under a

coconut tree, and spend relaxing evenings having drinks
with friends..."

At work, data, reports, and the sheer avalanche of information coming our
way is like the finger. It's an indication of something deeper, much like a
symptom is an indication of an underlying sickness. A useful skill in leadership (and management) is being able to absorb and digest this deluge of data
and then look *past* it to see what it means. Graphs, tables, and presentations
mean nothing in themselves—they are signs pointing to a greater truth. It's
the effective leaders who learn how to read the signs and respond to what
they *mean* rather than just what they say on the surface.

# Lesson

Try to look past the finger and see the moon. Many things in life are distracting and confusing, and many of us are chasing goals that we think will make us happy, but they are just "the finger." Look a little deeper and pursue the larger, more meaningful goals—"the moon." Keep the question, "What does it mean?" in the back of your mind as you go about your day to remind yourself to look past the surface and see more deeply.

# 49

🦴

# We Don't All Need to be Show Dogs

*The perils of being too professional*

I have been accused, at times, of being "too green." This doesn't mean someone thinks I'm overly environmentally conscious. It means that I apparently still have a lot to learn. At first I took this to heart, searching back over my dozen or so years of working in the corporate world and asking if maybe I had missed some valuable lessons, or not taken away enough from what I was exposed to. It was true that I hadn't spent countless hours with the captains of industry in back rooms wheeling and dealing. I hadn't masterminded multibillion dollar deals with Fortune 100 companies. Perhaps this lack of experience was a problem. To my critics, I hadn't yet earned my stripes. It was as if I'd stumbled in to an exclusive club house, and the few members there were looking down their nose through their reading glasses at me. *What are you doing here?*

Then it occurred to me that it wasn't necessarily *experience* that they thought I was missing. It was *approach*. By this, I think my detractors meant that I wasn't hardened, skeptical, and suspicious enough. I've always known I was good at reading people. Inherently I feel I knew who I can trust and who I should avoid. This internal guidance has always served me pretty well. This allows me the luxury to approach new situations with openness and trust. I maintain this trust until I confront hard evidence contradicting it.

In contrast, the advice I received was that I should approach new situations with distrust and suspicion until proven otherwise. The message was that people are out to screw you unless you keep your guard up. I, apparently, had not been around the block enough to learn this lesson.

Once I saw the criticism in this light, I felt much better. They were right; I hadn't yet become a hardened and calculating businessman. And I didn't want to. I didn't want to play in any arena where the entrance fee is your faith in other people, in humanity as a whole. That was a clubhouse that they could keep the keys to.

Dogs, like people, vary in their approach to others. For whatever reason—nature or nurture—my dogs naturally trust and love people. They have a healthy respect for strangers, but approach them with an attitude of "This guy is good until he shows me he's bad."[135] Other dogs I've seen at the park, and read about in the news, approach every unfamiliar person as a threat. Some dogs take months or more to win over. I feel bad for the dogs who live their whole lives in fear of the next shadow.

Is it true that there are bad people out there who set out to do harm to others? Absolutely. If you trust people might you get taken advantage

---

[135] There is an exception. They sometimes get set off by someone that they get a really bad vibe from. Usually I agree with their assessment.

of every once in a while? Sure. But the vast majority of people have good hearts and decent intentions. It's always good to trust, but verify. With this approach you can enjoy the benefits of pleasant unexpected developments while guarding—loosely—against personal harm.

Sometimes I think of the hardened outlook and what that must feel like. *The outside world is a threat. People are out to take advantage of me. I've got to get them before they get me.* Aside from the mental turmoil and physical stress this must create, it closes down opportunities. With these preconceived blinders on, life becomes a bit more restricted. Options that haven't been already considered and pre-approved are shut off. There's no room for spontaneity. The human brain can consciously only consider a handful of variables at once. More than three or four and it becomes overloaded. But think how many simultaneous variables our bodies deal with every second to remain functioning—thousands! Take it a step further and consider the variables impacting every situation we encounter. There are too many to count. How arrogant must we be to assume that we know better than nature[136] and can manipulate each situation to our own little advantage?

There is an unspoken connotation of the word "professional" with "serious" and "skeptical." To be "more professional," you are asked to give up your open, creative, and trusting side. *These foolish traits are better suited for children,* the professional says. *They are immature. To bring these qualities to the work world is to bring risk.*

I challenge this assumption. People respond to openness and creativity. They respond to trust. There is a saying that "If you want to be trusted, trust." The same goes for respect. What is gained by assuming the best about a person, and approaching them with this mindset, vastly outweighs the little bit of protection you get from being constantly skeptical and suspicious. Think of it this way: by being suspicious, you drive away both the bad in people but also the good. By being trusting and open, you may get stung once or twice, but you draw the good out in people all the time. Furthermore,

---

[136] Or the universe, or God, or the Dao…

by learning your lesson when you *are* stung, your intuition gets better and you reduce your future exposure to the bad element. But you get to keep the good.

Consider the energy that you have to expend to constantly guard against threats. It's exhausting just thinking about it. Imagine what else you could do with that energy. It's a shame that so many bright young people who want to advance their careers feel they have to shut down their playfulness and energy of youth, replacing it with a solemn expression and furrowed brow. Success and upward advancement don't mean that you have to dry up into an "experienced" shell.

Looking at how Paco and Zeke act, I'm inspired. They have the best approach: don't be naïve or foolish by running directly into danger, but don't carry the burden of suspicion with you forever. If you encounter someone who you get bad vibes from, or whom you realize is not trustworthy, simply move away from them. Disassociate yourself, and let them go on their (destructive) way.

After a little self-reflection, I'm proud of being "green." I consciously choose the path of openness and positive relationships with other people. I may miss out on opportunities to work with businesspeople who think I can't possibly know what I'm talking about if I bring this kind of energy. That's OK. There are plenty of other consultants who fit the traditional mold they are looking for.

# Lesson

You can be professional without being skeptical and hardened. Resist the pressure to become old before your time just because you think it may make you look more experienced. Keep an open and trusting approach to other people in your encounters. Keep your eyes open, and don't be foolish. But stay young at heart and trusting of people in general. This openness will encourage opportunities to come your way. And you can sit back and enjoy them, knowing that you didn't have to fight tooth and nail to get them like all the other "professionals."

# 50

ε—ჳ

# Animal Altruism
*Bringing together natural enemies*

Not a year goes by where I don't receive a forwarded e-mail about some animal that is raising another species of animal as her own. Usually it's a mama dog who has adopted some unusual baby animal that she otherwise would have no business hanging around with, from squirrels to ducks. A quick search of the news provides multiple examples, including a border collie who adopted a litter of kittens and a tiger mothering abandoned piglets!

In fact it seems that tiger cubs have a corner on the surrogate dog-mom market: a pit bull in Tunisia adopted two,[137] a golden retriever at the Kansas

---

[137] Dog adopts two tiger cubs 2007

zoo adopted three,[138] a dog in China adopts another three,[139] and my personal favorite: a dachshund in Germany parents a tiger cub.[140]

So what's all this about? Is it animal altruism? Universal maternal instinct? Whatever the reason the stories are popular and heartwarming. While not all leaders can be associated with this type of altruistic behavior, the best ones can effectively pull others into the fold. These types of leaders may not exactly be winning over other *species*, but from a business perspective they may as well be. Consider the construction CEO who brings together the internal accounting department and the jobsite superintendents. These two "animals" usually fight like cats and dogs. Just as impressive is the technology VP who seamlessly brings together sales and R&D directors toward a common goal.

By coordinating disparate elements and aligning their efforts, a leader can better work through others to accomplish common goals. She stays in constant and open communication with all parties, anticipating the differences in their perspectives to use them to her advantage. By framing events and goals in ways that each party will understand and appreciate, she creates meaning and motivation on all sides.

Take for example a mother who is mediating an argument between her teenage son and her husband on curfew time. The son wants no restrictions, while the father insists that he be home by 10:00 p.m. sharp or face punishment. The mother may feel that midnight is appropriate for her son, and she wants to work toward this compromise. Simply imposing her will probably will be ineffective. Instead, she asks questions of each side to see what their true objectives are. She finds that her husband is concerned that their son will be out all night running wild with no accountability. The son feels that any curfew indicates they don't trust him to make the right decisions. She asks her husband if he would feel better if his son checked in at 10:00 p.m. and

---

[138] Golden retriever adopts tiger cubs at zoo 2008
[139] Dog adopts tiger triplets 2007
[140] The cutest thing ever? Puppy dog adopts tiger cub n.d.

11:00 p.m. to let him know where he was and who he was with. He agrees that this would help. She then asks her son if he understands why they want to know that he's safe, and if he is willing to call twice to make them feel better. If he can do this, she explains, then they would feel better letting him stay out a bit later. He accedes. By working backward from differences to common ground, and then moving step-by-step forward by communicating clearly to each party, she has effectively led her team toward a common goal.

# Lesson

Don't just stick with your own kind and your own limited perspective. Take a chance to learn where others are coming from, and see if there isn't common ground on which you can meet and be productive. See if you can actively leave your comfort zone to work with someone from a completely different background. The better you can integrate your efforts, the more effective you can be at accomplishing goals. As you become comfortable doing this, you will be better able to bring others together to succeed.

# 51

&—3

# Gain Power by Giving It Away
*Power is not a finite resource*

It sounds unrealistic and overly altruistic to think about leaders giving away power. After all, the more you give away, the less you have for yourself, right? Wrong. Research has found that power is "an expandable pie, not a fixed sum; effective leaders do not see power as something that is competed for but rather as something that can be created and distributed to followers without detracting from their own power."[141]

If giving away power brings you more, why aren't more people doing it? Certainly when you enable your superior to succeed they are more likely to hold on to you and bring you with them up the ladder as they ascend. There's

[141] Kirkpatrick and Locke 1991

also an idea in business that the way to move up is to "replace yourself," to train the person who will take your position. In the process you will emerge as a leader yourself and build the organization beneath you.

But there may be more to it than that. Consider what would happen if you made everyone in your network more successful and powerful. You'd have more powerful friends and a more influential network, which increases your own power (never mind the principle of reciprocity where at least a few of those people will want to return the favor to you).

So the more you give, the more you get. Isn't this also the case with pets? I've heard many people offer up the excuse that now's not the right time to adopt a dog, that there isn't enough time, or enough money. In a few extreme cases this might be true. But for those who do invest in a dog, the rewards far outweigh the costs involved. Moving to Europe with Paco and Zeke was not easy or inexpensive. Even the dog food over there was ridiculously overpriced, and until we had a car we had to haul forty-pound bags of it back to our apartment on a bus. Not fun. But what we get out of owning them makes it all worth it.

# Lesson

Power is an expandable pie. The more you give away, the more there is overall to go around. Even though it can be a nuisance or a drain on energy to make others successful and increase their power, the returns to you can be significant. Effective leaders know how to create power and distribute it, so that their own power increases. While you're at it, invest in adopting a pet too. The cost and inconvenience will be worth the rewards you get in return.

# 52

ᘓᐽ

# Snap Out Of It and Go
# Throw a Ball

*Help people look beyond self-interest*

One of the best reasons to own a dog is to get your mind off of yourself for a few minutes each day. I can't tell you how many times I've be typing away on the computer, researching some idea or client strategy, when one of the dogs comes up and shoves his nose at my elbow. He wants to play. He wants attention. He wants me to *get off that stupid machine* and join the real world. It's a great reminder to take a break from whatever I'm doing, get on the floor, and roll around and play with him.

Sometimes I wonder what it looks like to Zeke when I'm working. There I sit, apparently not doing anything, staring at a thin box with a pale glow cast across my face—for hours. He must think I'm insane. As far as he knows, the computer is tremendously boring. It doesn't smell interesting (his reasoning for putting full attention toward an object). Nothing is moving. There aren't even any sounds coming from it but a faint clicking. I realize that maybe I *am* crazy to sit motionless like this, engrossed in pixels flickering before me.

A lot of our self-interest works the same way. There are so many commentaries and dialogues going on in our heads all the time that even if we are up and moving around we're still lost in self-absorption. Although we may go through the motions—washing dishes, driving, even carrying on a conversation—most of our attention is focused inwards. There's a constant commentary looping in our heads. We obsess over a comment someone made to us, critique decisions we made recently, judge another, plan for lunch, curse our luck, and dream for success.

My dogs are a constant reminder to break this spell and get some perspective. I put aside my self-interest and take Paco for a walk in the rain. Zeke and I wrestle on the floor as my computer waits ignored on the desk until it gives up on me and falls into hibernation mode. Paco engages me in tug of war with his blanket until shreds of it litter the room. These are moments of clarity, joy, and simple pleasures.

Sooner or later I return to my work, refreshed and settled. They really do me a favor, these furry little psychiatrists, by knowing just when I need to get out of my head. Unfortunately there aren't always dogs around. We have a responsibility to ourselves to break the self-absorbed spell we're under and play in the present moment. Leaders have the additional responsibility to pull others out as well.

We've seen that when we lead we work through others to accomplish common goals. Since everyone's first priority is their own self, leaders must realign an individual's efforts toward group objectives. This may be accomplished in any number of ways, from the use of rewards and deterrents to motivation and charisma. A leader is tasked with transforming the self-interest of many to the universal interest of the whole.

Moreover, there's another less obvious reason for leaders to help others look beyond their self-interest. When we see past our own small wants and needs, we gain perspective. With perspective comes wisdom. Think of lying on your back on a dark grassy hillside, staring up at a perfectly clear night sky filled with stars. Imagine it's so clear that you can see the Milky Way stretching across the firmament from horizon to horizon. As you consider the vastness of space and your tiny place in it, you detach from your little mental treadmill of wants and needs. A sense of peace and connection settles in, replacing the anxious commentary in your mind. You have a little perspective. Things are a little clearer, and decisions seem easier to make. The ability to bring others to this state is the gift of a talented leader.

# Lesson

The best leaders help others to look beyond short-sighted self-interest. To do this, one must first gain this perspective for himself. Take the time to be in the moment and leave your mental chatter behind. Play with your children. Throw the ball for your dogs. Dance around the kitchen with your spouse. These moments of spontaneous play are invaluable as they create space in your mind, which brings perspective and wisdom. Once you get the hang of it, encourage it in others. We'll all be better off for it.

# VI

# Parting Thoughts

Leadership study is gaining in popularity. Graduate programs are popping up, and leadership books sell like hotcakes (heck, maybe this one will too!). After all, who doesn't want to be a leader? In the race to improve ourselves and gain power and influence over others, it's important to stop and ask, *Where are we going with all this?*

This question allows us to step back from the details and gain some perspective. Why do we want to be leaders? Is our end goal just to beat out the other guy? Influence others? Get rich? For what purpose? What are we giving up along the way?

It should be clear by now that one of the foundations of leadership is context. What you do is no more important than how you do it, when and where it happens, and who you do it to. What works in some cases fails horribly in others. There is seldom only one right approach. However, with a healthy sense of questioning, optimistic skepticism, and sincere effort, progress can be made.

One of the reasons I like the subject of leadership is that it touches every situation and discipline. People all have goals, wants, and desires. We're all simply trying to be happier and to lead better lives. And like it or not, we're on this journey with other people. They're with us, against us, indifferent, or just in the way. If we know where we're going and we're capable of enlisting others to help us on our way, we'll get there faster.

It's also my hope that as a species we continue to recognize how inter-related we are. From casual observation, it appears that we're headed in that direction. Unending technological innovations break down more and more barriers between us as the years go on. This results in clashes and conflict but also agreement and integration. Individual goals seem more selfish when we realize we're all in the same boat.

Out of this recognition of interrelatedness springs the need to look internally to explore and make sense of the world. Once the gaze is directed internally, a difficult process of discovery begins. This journey, however challenging, provides significant benefits to the seeker as it unfolds before them. Perhaps it is stated best in the literature:

> Why must we go in and down? Because as we do so, we will meet the violence and terror that we carry within ourselves. If we do not confront these things inwardly, we will project them outward onto other people. When we have not understood that the enemy is within ourselves, we will find a thousand ways of making someone "out there" into the enemy.[142]

I've also noticed that the younger generations are much keener at detecting when another is being inauthentic or spouting BS. Perhaps it's because they've grown up in an age of unrelenting advertising and have developed the ability

---

[142] Palmer 1994

to separate the authentic from the disingenuous. Maybe the digital revolution has exposed how broken the current system really is and how hypocritical our politicians and other leaders can be. For whatever reason, I think it's wonderful. We need more authenticity to address the very real challenges we face, so we need more keen BS-detection skills and healthy skepticism.

In my own little way, I've brought this attitude to the world of consulting. My business model is simple. Treat every client as a real human being, not a source of income. Find out who they are, what they want, and what situation they're currently in. Work with them to find real and meaningful solutions so that they can move closer to their goals. Not everyone has the same end goals, or is in the same place along the way, so there isn't a one-size-fits-all solution. A consultant should be a "friend with expertise," a trusted advisor. He should be truly helpful.

My favorite metaphor about the uniqueness of each person's journey is that of a mountain. Picture a mountain with different terrain at every altitude and on each side. The north side is a forest with dense tall trees and no underbrush. The south side is thick with bushes and small shrubs. The eastern face is mostly exposed rock with slippery shale, while the west is covered with foggy fields littered with large boulders.

Now imagine each one of us is placed randomly somewhere on the mountain. I may be low on the north side, making my way through the forest with no visibility, while you may be high up on the east face cautiously scaling your way up a steep and slippery rock face. We all have the same goal—to reach the top. But everyone faces a different set of challenges depending on where they are. Now imagine we all have cell phones and can communicate freely with each other. If you and I talk, I might advise you that the fastest way up (in my experience) is by taking the steepest path up. It works for me, as I'm on a trail in the forest with no ability to see into the distance and with sure footing on my path. This advice would be absolutely wrong for you, as taking the steepest direct route up the rock face is the surest way to fall off the mountain and kill yourself. But I can't see your situation, and you can't see mine. I might think you're crazy for zigzagging your way up, and you might think I'm incompetent for taking the path I do.

The key here is to realize that while we may all have the same end goal in mind—reaching the summit—we have to take into consideration that we may not always know what's best for anyone else. Some advice is obvious and universal for everyone—for instance "pack enough food and water and sleep in a shelter"—while many pieces of advice may be unique to our own situations.

As you go out to improve yourself, keep these last three thoughts in mind. First, context is everything—there is no "right approach." Second, we're all in this together, so personal goals should mesh with common goals. Third, aim to be truly helpful. When others realize that you're genuine, they'll be happy to follow you anywhere. Finally, strive to be more than just capable. Lead to the fullest of your capacity:

> Living, working, and leading based on our capacity means using our whole selves, including intellectual, emotional, and spiritual abilities and understandings. A broad literature has emphasized that being a whole person means operating from the mind, heart, spirit, and body...[143]

...like dogs do.

---

[143] Daft 2005

# Epilogue: Zeke's Last Lesson

While this book was in its final stages before going to print, something very sad happened. Zeke, who had just spent the weekend on Cape Cod with my parents while we were out of state at a wedding, got very ill. Despite a long weekend of frolicking, beach walks, and meeting new people, he collapsed in a heap when I took him back to our house in Boston. On his back, sides, neck, and chest I found large hard bumps about the size of a fingertip. He had barely eaten while away, and his skin stretched tight over visible ribs and a hollow belly. His face was drawn and when I sat down with him on the floor he gave me a very long and sad look. It looked like cancer.

We immediately called our vet and got him an appointment the next day, hoping for the best. They took x-rays and blood and told us that he had quite a bit of fluid in his lungs. It was certain he had pneumonia. But the vet didn't know what to make of the bumps. They weren't tumors, she explained, but hard pockets of pus. A sample was taken and sent to the lab and results would come in the morning. Michaele took him home with a prescription for antibiotics and a heavy heart. That night I happened to be out of town on a two-day business trip, and regretted that I couldn't be with them. Zeke, who usually is not allowed in the bed, took my place overnight and passed out next to Michaele.

As I was running through the Houston terminal to catch a connection the next morning, I got the call. Michaele told me through tears that Zeke had contracted blastomycosis, very rare fungal infection in his lungs, and it had spread into other parts of his body. While common in the Southeastern states and Canada, the infection was unheard of in Massachusetts. Apparently Zeke - our little Ferdinand who loved sniffing the flowers - had inhaled the spores at some point out of some rotting earth. Who knows how long it had been incubating.

The vet told us that his chances weren't good. The infection was very advanced. We were given the options of euthanizing him immediately, taking him home to let the sickness take him on its own time, or bringing him to a 24-hour veterinary hospital. We rushed him into the Massachusetts Veterinary Referral Hospital where he was admitted for 48 hours. While they made him comfortable and ran more tests, we raced to the internet to read up on blastomycosis.

As with any topic online, information was varied. On a forum dedicated to supporting those dealing with the disease I read of dogs who had died suddenly, some who had recovered completely, and others who had pulled through with lost legs, eyes, and other disabilities. In the best case, recovery was long. If he pulled through, Zeke would need to be quarantined in our house away from Paco and encouraged against his will to eat not only food but two pills a day for at least a year. There was a good chance he would die anyway, even after three or six months, from a relapse. If he did die, it would be from suffocation as his lungs filled up with blood.

I rushed home from Texas and went straight from the airport to the hospital to see him. I found him in his cage in the intensive care room. He had just been put on oxygen and was lying with an oversized clear plastic cone on his head. As I said hello with a cracked voice and sat down next to him, all around us dogs in anguish wailed and yipped and howled in unending waves of sorrow. Zeke lay quietly through it all, IV in his leg, breathing heavily. The doctor came and told me that now was the worst part; the antifungal medication was very hard on a dog's system for the first two days. An ophthalmologist's report had just come back from the lab indicating the spread of infectious spores to his eyes. He struggled to open them to look at me.

We sat there for an hour together. I stroked his bumpy body and told him he was a good boy while he slept in a half-stupor. Once or twice he lifted his head suddenly and in a fit sneezed blood out through his nose and mouth, spraying the inside of the cone and the surrounding blankets. The bumps had started to break into open wounds. It was bad.

At closing I left with a promise by the staff that they would call me if his condition changed, even in the middle of the night. We'd look at his condition tomorrow morning. The next morning we were told that he was getting worse. More lesions had formed, and he could not be taken off oxygen. We could keep him there another week, we were told, but there were no promises he would make it and at the end of that week of suffering we'd be back in the same position as today.

In one of the hardest decisions we've made, we knew it was time to put him down. Keeping him around just for our own benefit would be selfish. But he would have done it. He would have endured more pain just to comfort us. That was Zeke. But we couldn't allow that.

We drove the twenty minutes in stunned silence to see him. After a short wait he staggered down the hall towards us in a haze. When he saw us and heard our voices he wagged his little tail. Despite all the pain he was still glad to see us. They led us to a visiting room where Zeke hesitated at the door. Maybe he was out of breath. Maybe he was exhausted. Or maybe he knew at some level that this was the end. Then he limped through the door and into our waiting arms.

We drove his little body, wrapped in blankets, to my parents' property on Cape Cod where he had been joyously playing just a short six days earlier. Low, steel-grey clouds hung in the sky, periodically pelting large droplets of rain on our windshield. We dug a deep hole for him on the side of a hill next to the garden, where he had loved to wander around sniffing.

The skies opened up and soaked Michaele, me, and my parents to the bone. No one cared. We each threw a handful of dirt onto the small bundled package that until that morning had been our little buddy. He was buried with his favorite toy, a little blue rubber dog, nestled next to his head. After a final goodbye, we slogged back through rain to the house to get Paco.

So what's Zeke's final lesson? What can this whole painful ordeal possibly teach us? I know many thoughts went through my head, and continue to do so. Surely life is short and uncertain. Zeke was never afraid, never complained. He endured what must have been great pain and stayed loyal and committed to us. He even comforted us when we were upset and *he* was the dying one. He brought love to everyone he met, and brought out that love from them in return. Even the nurse, who had known him for only hours, told us "This dog IS love." The decision we made was so heartbreaking, but we knew it was our responsibility. Choosing the moment to let him go was a terrible privilege. It was both a blessing and a curse at the same time.

I don't know what Zeke's final lesson is. It may be something different for each one of us. I know I learned a lot about love, loyalty, companionship, making the right decision even though it may be the hardest one, the uncertainty that we face every day when we wake up, and gratitude. I saw that despite his pain and late-stage illness he gave it all he had that last weekend on Cape Cod and thoroughly enjoyed himself, cashing in what little energy he had left and bringing happiness, as always, to everyone.

I can't tell you what you should take away from this last sad story. You'll have to decide for yourself. After all, leaders can't have all the answers given to them.

# About the Author

Andrew Krüger earned his Masters in Leadership and graduated with a Distinguished Scholar Award from Boston University, an MBA in Organizational Behavior and Management from Tulane University, and degrees in Economics and Cultural Anthropology from Colgate University. He has spent over seven years teaching and consulting to small businesses in the US and Europe, and is currently the Managing Partner of Krüger Strategy Group, LLC. He blogs about leadership topics on makingthehippodance. blogspot.com, and lives with his wife and dog in Boston, Massachusetts.

# Bibliography

"teaspout". *Home*. March 5, 2008. http://www.teaspout.com/?p=271 (accessed April 5, 2011).

Alexander, John. *Consensus: Hidden Codes of Swedish Leadership*. Stockholm, Sweden: John Alexander AB, 2008.

Bass, B. M. *Handbook of Leadership*. New York: The Free Press, 1990.

Bowers, David G., and Stanley E. Seashore. "Predicting organizational effectiveness with a four-factor theory of leadership." *Administrative Science Quarterly*, 1966: 238-263.

Burke, P. J. "Authority relations and descriptive behavior in small discussion groups." *Sociometry*, 1966: 237-250.

Chodron, Pema. *Start Where You Are*. Boston: Shambhala Publications, Inc., 1994.

Clements, Christine, and John B. Washbush. "The Two Faces of Leadership: Considering the Dark Side of Leader-Follower Dynamics." *Journal of Workplace Learning*, 1999: 170-175.

Coleridge, Samuel Taylor. "Rime of the Ancient Mariner." In *Lyrical Ballads*, by Samuel Taylor Coleridge and William Wordsworth. 1798.

Conger, Jay A. "The dark side of leadership." *Organizational Dynamics*, 1990: 44-55.

Daft, Richard. *The Leadership Experience, 4th ed.* Mason, OH: Thomson Learning Academic Resource Center, 2005.

De Cremer, David, and Daan van Knippenberg. "Leader Self-sacrifice and Leadership Effectiveness." *Organizational Behavior and Human Decision Processes*, 2004: 140-155.

Dirks, Kurt T. "Trust in Leadership and Team Performance." *Journal of Applied Psychology 85*, 2000: 1004-1012.

*Dog adopts tiger triplets.* 5 18, 2007. http://www.guardian.co.uk/world/2007/may/18/china.davidbatty (accessed 3 5, 2011).

*Dog Adopts Two Tiger Cubs.* May 22, 2007. http://www.cbsnews.com/video/watch/?id=2836533n (accessed 3 5, 2011).

Eagley, Alice H., and Blair T. Johnson. "Gender and leadership style." *Psychological Bulletin 108*, 1990: 233-256.

Eisenhower, Dwight D. *Dwight D. Eisenhower Quotes.* http://www.brainyquote.com/quotes/quotes/d/dwightdei149098.html (accessed 4 25, 2011).

Ford, Henry. *Select Henry Ford Quotations.* 1937. http://www.brainyquote.com/quotes/quotes/h/henryford145978.html (accessed 5 16, 2011).

French Jr., John R. P., and Bertram Raven. "The Bases of Social Power." In *Studies in Social Power*, by D. Cartwright, 150-167. Ann Arbor, MI: Institute for Social Research, 1959.

Gallo, Carmine. *The Presentation Secrets of Steve Jobs: How to be Insanely Great in Front of Any Audience.* McGraw Hill, 2010.

Gardner, Howard. *Leading Minds.* New York, NY: BasicBooks, 1995.

George, J. M. "Emotions and Leadership: The Role of Emotional Intelligence." *Human Relations*, 2000: 1027-1055.

*Golden retriever adopts tiger cubs at zoo.* July 31, 2008. http://www.msnbc.msn. com/id/25945650/ns/technology_and_science-science/ (accessed 3 5, 2011).

Greene, Charles N. "The reciprocal nature of influence between leader and subordinate." *Journal of Applied Psychology 60*, 1975: 187-193.

Hagan, Steve. *Buddhism Plain and Simple.* New York, NY: Broadway Books, 1998.

Hollander, Edwin. "Leadership, Followership, Self, and Others." *Leadership Quarterly*, 1992: 43-54.

House, R. J., and P. M. Podsakoff. "Leader effectiveness." In *Organizational Behavior: The State of Science*, by J. (ed.) Greenberg, 628-641. Hillsdale, NJ: Erlbaum, 1994.

Hughes, Richard L., Robert C. Ginnett, and Gordon J. Curphy. In *Leadership: Enhancing the Lessons of Experience, 6th ed.*, by Richard L. Hughes, Robert C. Ginnett and Gordon J. Curphy, 239-245. Boston: McGraw Hill, 2009.

Judge, Timothy A., Remus Ilies, Joyce E. Bono, and Megan W. Gerhardt. "Personality and Leadership: a Qualitative and Quantitative Review." *Journal of Applied Psychology 87*, 2002: 765-780.

Kafka, Franz. *Parables and Paradoxes.* Schocken Books, 1961.

Kennedy, Robert F. *Remarks of Senator Robert F. Kennedy to the Cleveland City Club, Cleveland, Ohio, April 5, 1968.* April 5, 1968. http://www.jfklibrary. org/Research/Ready-Reference/RFK-Speeches/Remarks-of-Senator-Robert-F-Kennedy-to-the-Cleveland-City-Club-Cleveland-Ohio-April-5-1968.aspx (accessed 8 7, 2011).

Kent, Russel L., and Sherry E. Moss. "Effects of sex and gender role on leader emergence." *Academy of Management Journal*, 1994: 1335-1346.

Kirkpatrick, S. A., and E. A. Locke. "Leadership: Do Traits Matter?" *Academy of Management Executive*, 1991: 48-60.

Larson, Gary. ""What we say to dogs and what they hear"." *Cartoon.*

Ledru-Rollin, Alexandre Auguste. *Leadership Quotations*. 2002. http://www.inspirational-quotes.info/leadership.html (accessed 6 14, 2011).

Locke, E. A., N. Cartledge, and C. S. Knerr. "Studies of the relationship between satisfaction, goal setting, and performance." *Organizational Behavior and Human Performance*, 1970: 135-158.

Mavis, Mary. "Painless performance evaluations." *Training and Development*, 1994: 40-44.

Mehrabian, Albert. *Silent Messages.* Belmont, CA: Wadsworth, 1971.

Newton, Isaac. *Principia, vol. 1.* 1729.

Norman, W.T. "Toward an Adequate Taxonomy of Personality Attributes: Replicated Factor Structure in Peer Nomination Personality Ratings." *Journal of Abnormal Social Psychology* 66, 1963: 574-583.

Palmer, P.J. "Leading from within: out of the shadows, into the light." In *Spirit at work: Discovering the Spirituality in Leadership*, by J. A. (ed.) Conger. San Francisco, CA: Jossey-Bass, 1994.

Pease, Barbara, and Allan Pease. *The Definitive Book of Body Language.* New York, NY: Bantam Books, 2006.

Pierce, Jon L., and John W. Newstrom. *Leaders & The Leadership Process, 5th ed.* Boston: McGraw-Hill Irwin, 2008.

Porrill, Ward. *The Best Academy Award speeches of all time.* 2 10, 2010. http://www.examiner.com/movie-awards-in-national/the-best-academy-awards-speeches-of-all-time (accessed 4 21, 2011).

—. *The Worst Academy Award speeches of all time.* 2 5, 2010. http://www.examiner.com/movie-awards-in-national/the-worst-academy-award-speeches-of-all-time (accessed 4 21, 2011).

Rensselaer Polytechnic Institute, Lally School of Management and Technology. "Emotional Intelligence and Earning Power." *Businessweek Frontier*, 2 5, 2001: F4.

Saban, Lewis. *Quotations about the Dog.* 6 14, 2007. http://www-hsc.usc.edu/~rneville/sayings.html (accessed 5 10, 2011).

Salancik, Gerald R., and Jeffrey Pfeffer. "Who gets power- and how they hold on to it." *Organizational Dynamics*, 2005: 3-21.

Scandura, Terri A. "Rethinking Leader-Member Exchange." *Leadership Quarterly*, 1999: 25-40.

Schelling, T. "The ecology of micromotives." *Public Interest*, 1971: 61-98.

Selznick, P. *Leadership in administration.* Evanston, IL: Row, Peterson, 1957.

Shera, Jesse. "Librarianship and information science." In *The study of information: interdisciplinary messages*, by Fritz Machlup and Una Mansfield. New York: John Wiley and Sons, 1983.

Sivers, Derek. "Derek Sivers: How to Start a Movement." *Ted.com.* February 2010. http://www.ted.com/talks/lang/eng/derek_sivers_how_to_start_a_movement.html (accessed April 5, 2011).

Smircich, Linda, and Gareth Morgan. "Leadership: the management of meaning." *Journal of Applied Behavioral Science*, 1982: 257-273.

Stogdill, R. M. "Personal Factors with Leadership: A Survey of the Literature." *Journal of Psychology 28*, 1948: 35-71.

Tapia, M. "Measuring Emotional Intelligence." *Psychological Reports*, 2001: 353-364.

*The cutest thing ever? Puppy dog adopts tiger cub.* http://www.dailymotion.com/video/x9cqek_the-cutest-thing-every-puppy-dog-ad_fun (accessed 3 5, 2011).

Tupes, E.C., and R.E. Christal. *Recurrent Personality Factors Based on Trait Ratings.* Lackland Air Force Base, TX U.S. Air Force: Technical Report ASD-TR-61-97, 1961.

unknown. *Finger Pointing at the Moon.* 11 16, 2007. http://www.storiesofwisdom.com/finger-pointing-at-the-moon/ (accessed 5 18, 2010).

—. *The Consultant and the Fisherman.* 5 15, 2011. http://storiesfortrainers.com/theconsultantandthefisherman.aspx (accessed 6 20, 2011).

Van Velsor, Ellen, Cynthia D. McCauley, and Marian N. Ruderman. *Handbook of Leadership Development.* SAn Francisco, CA: Jossey-Bass, 2010.

Wolff, S. B., A. T. Pescosolide, and V. U. Druskat. "Emotional Intelligence as the Basis of Leader Language in Self-Managing Teams." *Leadership Quarterly*, 2002: 505-522.

www.ingramcontent.com/pod-product-compliance
Lightning Source LLC
Chambersburg PA
CBHW060542200326
41521CB00007B/447